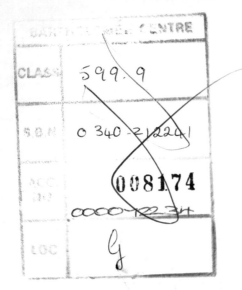

the human body

a blueprint of Man's structure and function

the human body

a blueprint of Man's structure and function

C. H. BARNETT
H. GRAYSHON LUMBY
DERYCK TAVERNER

HODDER AND STOUGHTON

LONDON   SYDNEY   AUCKLAND   TORONTO

ISBN 0 340 21224 1

First printed 1966. Reprinted (with revisions) 1968
First printed in this format 1968
Reprinted 1970, 1972, 1975
Limp Edition 1976
Reprinted 1978, 1981

Printed in Hong Kong for
Hodder and Stoughton Educational,
a division of Hodder and Stoughton Ltd,
Mill Road, Dunton Green, Sevenoaks, Kent TN13 2YD,
by Colorcraft Ltd.

6690 AB1 LCLL4

contents

Page

v

introduction

An architect planning a large factory must bear in mind:-

1. The materials required for its construction and upkeep.

2. The internal organisation, including the maintenance services, communications, heating, water supply and drainage.

3. The intended product.

The human body can be compared to a chemical factory in many respects and we have accordingly divided this book into three sections:-

1. The materials of the human body.

2. The organisation and arrangement of the body.

3. The product of the human body.

Some of these matters can be explained almost entirely in pictures, but others need description. We have tried to strike a balance between pictures and text so that the reader can visualise the essential features of the living human body, just as he can picture workings of a factory by studying an architect's blueprint.

section one the materials of the human body

The fundamental components of all living things are chemicals linked together in a most complicated way.

the
materials
of the
human body

This material is arranged in separate units, the *cells,* which vary greatly in size.

The cells are grouped together in very large numbers to form *tissues* – for example, fat, cartilage (gristle), muscle (flesh) and bone.

The tissues are assembled together to form *organs,* each with special functions, working in harmony to form the living body.

[4]

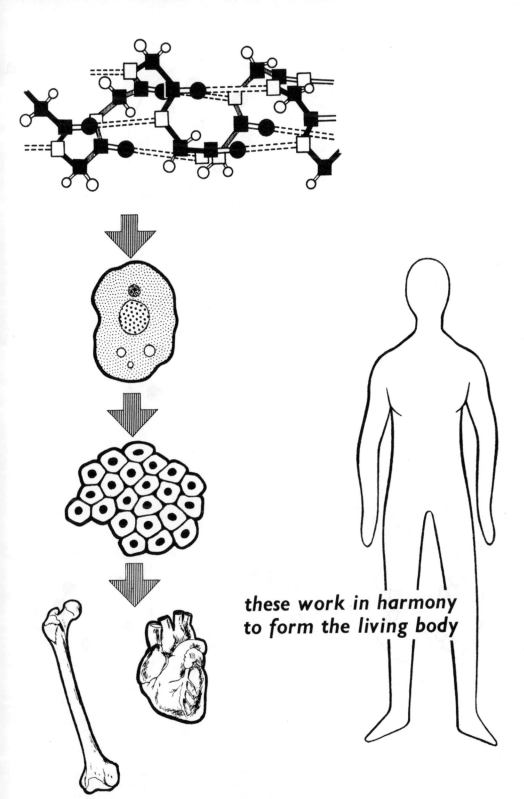

*these work in harmony
to form the living body*

An elementary account of the chemistry of
matter is an essential preliminary to a proper
understanding of the chemistry of the body.

All materials (chemical substances) are composed of small units – the *atoms* – which cannot be split up without altering the nature of the substance. If all the atoms in a certain substance are the same it is called an *element*.

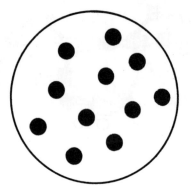

Elements are often found mixed together; air is a *mixture* of two elements, oxygen and nitrogen.

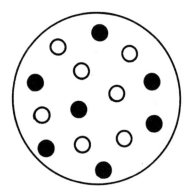

Many substances consist of the atoms of several elements linked together. They are *compounds* and the cluster of combined atoms is called a *molecule*.

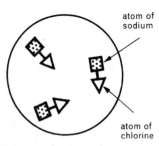

atom of sodium

atom of chlorine

Molecules of sodium chloride (common salt)

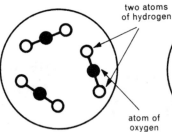

two atoms of hydrogen

atom of oxygen

Molecules of water

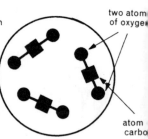

two atoms of oxygen

atom carbon

Molecules of carbon dioxide

Some other elements are iron, calcium, phosphorus, sulphur and iodine. In medicine these are often referred to as *minerals*. Their simple compounds with each other are called *salts*.

The composition of molecules can be indicated by *chemical formulae* in which capital letters stand for the atoms and figures show the number of each kind of atom in the molecule.

For example, the sugar glucose is written $C_6 H_{12} O_6$ because each molecule contains 6 carbon, 12 hydrogen and 6 oxygen atoms.

Similarly, water is written $H_2 O$

and carbon dioxide $C O_2$

Glycerine (called glycerol by chemists to indicate its relationship to alcohol) is
$$C_3 H_8 O_3$$

It is more informative to indicate the pattern of the atoms in a large molecule and glycerol is better represented as:—

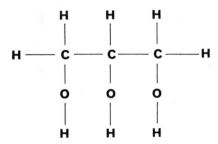

Some substances are made up of very large molecules. A type of starch found in the liver is called *glycogen*. Its large molecule is formed by linkages between many smaller, identical molecules:—

$$(C_6 H_{10} O_5)-(C_6 H_{10} O_5)-(C_6 H_{10} O_5)-$$

the chemistry of

All living things, animals or plants, contain three main
types of chemical substances: *carbohydrates, fats* and
proteins. They also contain a large amount of water and
small amounts of certain minerals.

carbohydrates and fats

Contain three elements only.

Carbon   Oxygen   Hydrogen

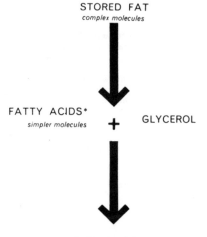

STORED FAT
complex molecules

All living things use carbohydrates as their source of
energy. Reserves are usually
stored as *starch* in plants and
glycogen in animals. Fats are
also stored in animals. When
fat stores are being used up
they are broken down like this:—

FATTY ACIDS*   **+**   **GLYCEROL**
simpler molecules

further breakdown

*Acids *are sour substances, like vinegar, that turn blue litmus paper red.*

CARBON DIOXIDE **+** **ENERGY** **+** WATER

living things

Large amounts of many different proteins are contained in every cell. They all have extremely large molecules, hundreds of times the size of a glucose molecule. Most proteins form part of the bodies of cells but some lie elsewhere—for example, in the spaces between the cells.

proteins

contain at least four elements.

'Carbon

Oxygen

Hydrogen

Nitrogen

Proteins can also be used as sources of energy.

Proteins are essential to life so that small amounts have to be taken into the body regularly to replace the protein broken down during living processes.

PROTEIN
very complex molecules

urea

simpler substance containing nitrogen

discarded by body in urine

AMINO ACIDS

simpler molecules

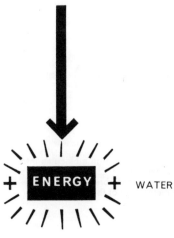

CARBON DIOXIDE + ENERGY + WATER

minerals

The proper working of the body, especially the nerves and muscles, depends upon the correct balance and amount of minerals in the body fluids. Calcium and phosphorus are needed for bone formation.

enzymes

Most chemical changes in the home are produced by the action of heat, as in cooking, but the chemistry of living things must take place at body temperature. Enzymes are needed for this. They are special protein molecules which can facilitate chemical changes without being used up themselves. Each enzyme is responsible for a single step in a chemical process and complicated changes require many different enzymes acting in the correct order. There are many thousands of different enzymes in the human body.

Some enzymes build large molecules out of small ones (a process called *synthesis*). For example,

many glucose molecules   a glycogen molecule

water as a by product

Other enzymes break down large molecules into small ones. All the varied chemical changes involved in synthesis and breakdown are referred to as the *metabolism* of the body.

The chemical substances needed by the body are derived from the *oxygen* of the air and from *food*, which consists of dead animals and plants or their products. All chemical processes produce *waste products* and in the body these are discharged into the *urine* or into the *air* as carbon dioxide. Useless matter taken into the body with the food is discharged in the *faeces*. The energy produced in the body emerges in several ways:

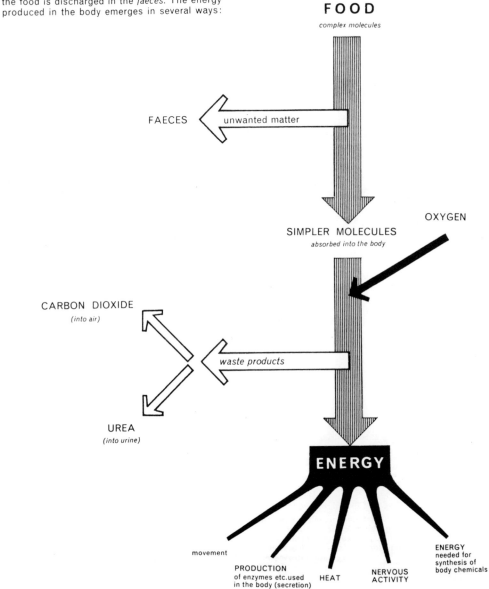

FOOD
complex molecules

FAECES unwanted matter

SIMPLER MOLECULES
absorbed into the body

OXYGEN

CARBON DIOXIDE
(into air)

waste products

UREA
(into urine)

ENERGY

movement

PRODUCTION
of enzymes etc.used
in the body (secretion)

HEAT

NERVOUS
ACTIVITY

ENERGY
needed for
synthesis of
body chemicals

to maintain life the human body needs :—

water
food
minerals
vitamins

water

INPUT

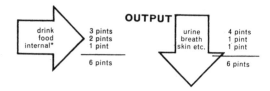

		OUTPUT	
drink	3 pints	urine	4 pints
food	2 pints	breath	1 pint
internal*	1 pint	skin etc.	1 pint
	6 pints		6 pints

Internal water is produced by the chemical processes of the body (page 9)

food

A knowledge of the
composition of foods is
essential to the production
of efficient and economical
diets.

cost	body requirements	use in body	
CHEAP	½ lb.	for energy	CARBOHYDRATE
EXPENSIVE	2-4 oz.	for energy	FAT
EXPENSIVE	2-4 oz.	for growth and replacement	PROTEIN

minerals

The chief minerals in the body are sodium, potassium, iron, calcium, phosphorus, magnesium, chlorine, sulphur and iodine but traces of others are required. The ordinary mixed diet contains adequate quantities of them but additional minerals may sometimes be needed. In the tropics excessive loss of sodium and chlorine must be replaced and extra iodine may be needed when living far from the sea.

nutrition

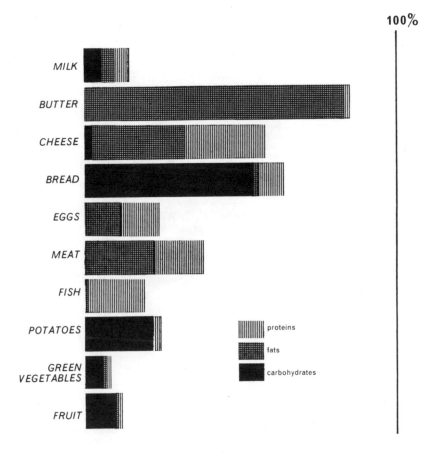

100%

MILK

BUTTER

CHEESE

BREAD

EGGS

MEAT

FISH

POTATOES

GREEN
VEGETABLES

FRUIT

|||||||| proteins

▦ fats

■ carbohydrates

vitamins

type	source	required for
A	Milk, liver	Cell growth and replacement. Good vision, especially at night.
B complex	Milk, meat, yeast, liver	Healthy skin, nervous system, intestine and blood.
C	Fresh vegetables and fruit	Strong blood vessels. Prevention of scurvy.
D	Eggs, milk, butter, liver	Calcium absorption. Prevention of rickets.

[13]

Cells contain a sticky, watery solution of minerals, proteins, fats and carbohydrates which is too delicate to survive unprotected.

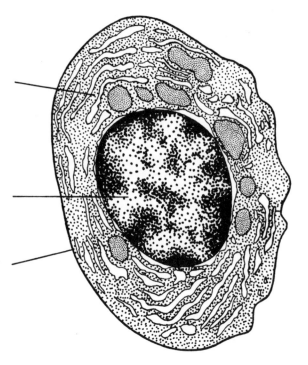

All the work of the cell is done in this spongy material. It contains complicated membranes and bodies made of protein, where the enzyme-controlled chemical processes take place.

The nucleus is a complex mass of protein which controls the activity of the whole cell because it directs and organises all the enzymes in the cell.

The membrane encloses the cell and protects it from its environment.

Cells are minute chemical factories in which elaborate chemical processes controlled by enzymes are constantly building up and breaking down chemical substances. Water moves freely throughout the whole body structure but substances dissolved and suspended in water are held up in varying amount by the membranes surrounding the cells. These membranes have numerous small holes which allow water to pass but delay particles according to their size. There are therefore different amounts of minerals, fats, proteins and carbohydrates inside and outside the cells. The maintenance of these differences is essential to health and many of the activities of the cells are devoted to this purpose.

cells

There are profound differences between cells. Some cells are small in size and relatively simple in structure and function – the red cells of the blood. These do not even possess a nucleus, hence they are better termed *red corpuscles*. Others are twenty times as big and have a complicated nuclear structure – the female reproductive cell or *ovum*. There are cells in the wall of the stomach which serve only to make acid for digesting food, while there are cells in the liver which perform multiple actions in the handling and storage of food substances.

in summary

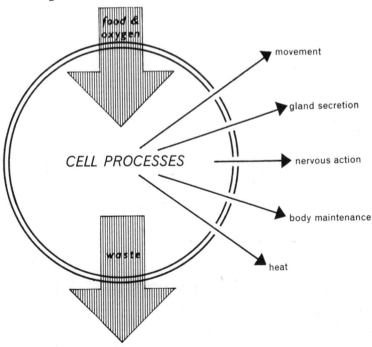

body fluids

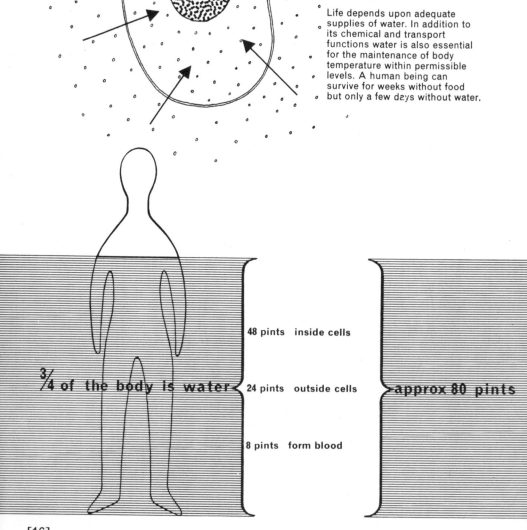

All cells contain water and are surrounded by *tissue fluid* containing various amounts of water. Water is the essential medium in which the chemical processes of the body take place and serves as the transport link for the movement of materials everywhere in the body.

Life depends upon adequate supplies of water. In addition to its chemical and transport functions water is also essential for the maintenance of body temperature within permissible levels. A human being can survive for weeks without food but only a few days without water.

¾ of the body is water

48 pints   inside cells

24 pints   outside cells

8 pints   form blood

approx 80 pints

Tissue fluid and *blood,* the special fluid that circulates throughout the body, form the principal body fluids. They contain fats, carbohydrates, proteins and minerals either dissolved or suspended in water. There is free movement of all these substances, except protein,

between blood and tissue fluid but **NOT** between tissue fluid and the cells.

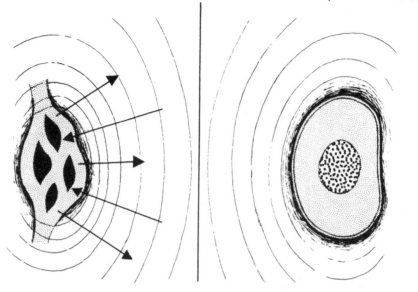

All bodily traffic – the exchange of gases, minerals, food and waste products – takes place through the body fluids. The water in cells changes slowly, but the water in the blood and tissue fluid is continually changing and mixing, spreading and moving supplies and waste products all over the body.

diffusion

Diffusion is an essential process which occurs automatically. Gas released in a room or dye dropped into water soon spread to fill the whole available space by the process of diffusion. If a sheet with tiny holes – a porous membrane – is stretched across a bowl of water it will block the passage of any dye particles which are too large to pass through the holes. If there is more dye on one side of the membrane than the other, water automatically passes from the weak solution to the strong side, so that the strengths of the dye solutions on the two sides of the membrane tend to become equal. The force moving the water from the weak to the strong side of the membrane is called *osmotic pressure.* Diffusion and osmotic pressure are of the utmost importance to the functioning of the human body because it contains billions of porous membranes in and around its cells.

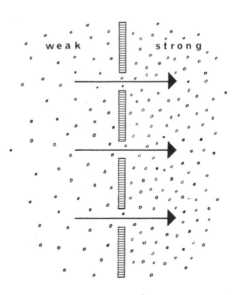

weak   strong

arrangement
of cells

*Cells are of many shapes and sizes. Those of a particular
type are usually collected together to form* tissues:-

a. covering tissues,
b. connective tissues,
c. special tissues.

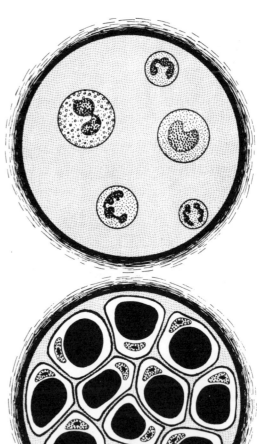

If there is ample space between the
cells they are often rounded in form
as in this group of well-spaced white
blood cells.

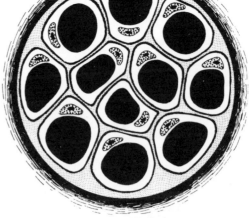

Usually the cells are closely packed
together and their shapes are
affected as in this lump of fat. Note
the droplet of fat stored in each cell,
pushing the nucleus to one side.

Often several tissues are built up into complicated organs
which have one or more special functions in the body.

Cells are often arranged in sheets that cover or line organs.
Some examples are :—

A thin sheet of flattened cells forming a smooth surface for an organ – the *pleura* over the lungs.

A rolled-up thin sheet forming a smooth lining for a tube – the inner lining of an artery.

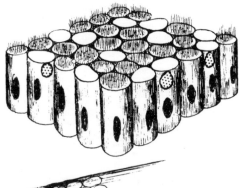

A thick sheet formed of a single layer of tall columnar cells – some producing globules of sticky *mucus* and others bearing small moving "bristles" which brush material over the surface – the mucous membrane lining the nose.

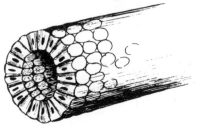

A rolled-up thick sheet of cells which lines a tube and pours mucus into it – the lining of the last part of the food tube (the *rectum*).

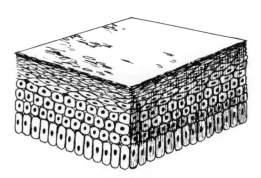

A many-layered sheet with flattened dead cells on the surface that can be worn away harmlessly – the *skin*.

connective tissues

Connective Tissues
In these the cells are widely spaced. The
material between the cells is called
matrix.

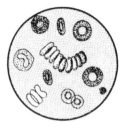

Examples:—
BLOOD
Fluid matrix called *plasma*.

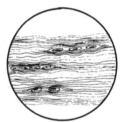

LOOSE FIBROUS TISSUE
Found around and between organs. A soft
matrix contains strand-like fibres some of which
are white and give strength while others are
yellow and give elasticity.

SIMPLE CARTILAGE
Cells set in a pale blue matrix, easily bent.
Example: in the flexible part of the nose.

FIBROCARTILAGE
Simple cartilage with fibres in its matrix to give
toughness. Example: the discs between the
spinal vertebrae.

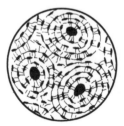

BONE
Cells set in matrix strengthened by chemicals
similar to limestone, containing calcium and
phosphorus. Blood percolates through bone,
nourishing the bone cells, through narrow
channels which penetrate the rigid matrix.

some special tissues

muscular tissues

This has the special ability to shorten – *contraction*. There are three types:—

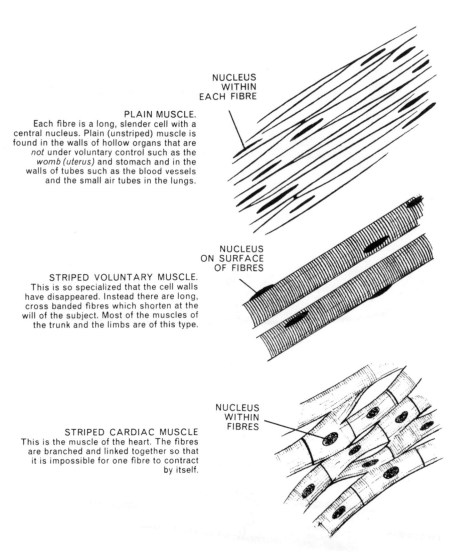

NUCLEUS
WITHIN
EACH FIBRE

PLAIN MUSCLE.
Each fibre is a long, slender cell with a central nucleus. Plain (unstriped) muscle is found in the walls of hollow organs that are *not* under voluntary control such as the *womb (uterus)* and stomach and in the walls of tubes such as the blood vessels and the small air tubes in the lungs.

NUCLEUS
ON SURFACE
OF FIBRES

STRIPED VOLUNTARY MUSCLE.
This is so specialized that the cell walls have disappeared. Instead there are long, cross banded fibres which shorten at the will of the subject. Most of the muscles of the trunk and the limbs are of this type.

NUCLEUS
WITHIN
FIBRES

STRIPED CARDIAC MUSCLE
This is the muscle of the heart. The fibres are branched and linked together so that it is impossible for one fibre to contract by itself.

some special tissues (cont.)

nervous tissue

Nervous tissue. The special cells which transmit the signals from one part of the body to another are called *neurones*. They are surrounded by smaller cells – *neuroglia* – which support and nourish them. There is very little tissue fluid in brain and spinal cord.

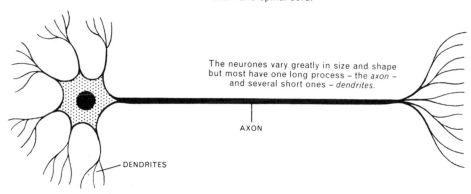

The neurones vary greatly in size and shape but most have one long process – the *axon* – and several short ones – *dendrites*.

AXON

DENDRITES

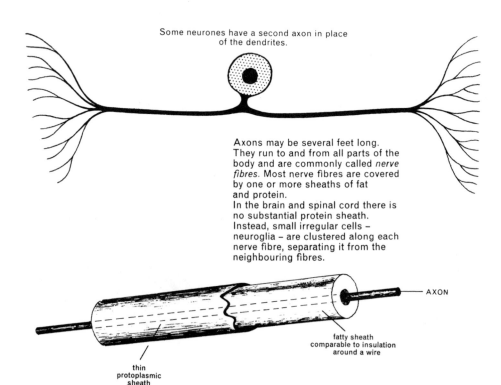

Some neurones have a second axon in place of the dendrites.

Axons may be several feet long. They run to and from all parts of the body and are commonly called *nerve fibres*. Most nerve fibres are covered by one or more sheaths of fat and protein.
In the brain and spinal cord there is no substantial protein sheath. Instead, small irregular cells – neuroglia – are clustered along each nerve fibre, separating it from the neighbouring fibres.

AXON

fatty sheath
comparable to insulation
around a wire

thin
protoplasmic
sheath

Organs. *Complicated organs are built up of different tissues, which together perform one or more specialised functions.*

organs

A few organs are solid. The tongue consists of bundles of striped voluntary muscle fibres interspersed with blood vessels and covered by several layers of cells.

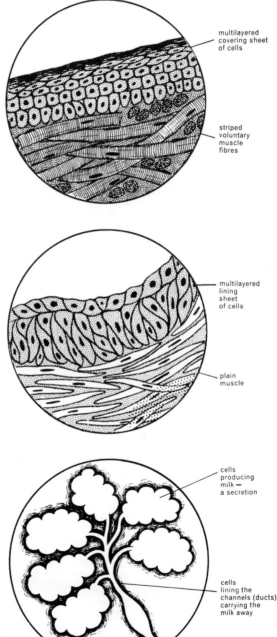

multilayered covering sheet of cells

striped voluntary muscle fibres

Many organs are hollow. The bladder consists of sheets of plain muscle fibres with a lining of cells.

multilayered lining sheet of cells

plain muscle

Some contain tubes. The breast consists of clusters of cells producing milk, which is led away to the nipple by a complex system of branching tubes called *ducts*.

Milk is a secretion of the breast. Any organ producing a secretion which has a useful function is called a gland.

cells producing milk — a secretion

cells lining the channels (ducts) carrying the milk away

section two the organisation of the human body

living cells work best when the temperature, humidity, acidity and mineral content of their surroundings are kept steady. The maintenance of this "steady state" is described in this section.

the organization
of the human body

Organs rarely work alone. Usually they work together as members of Systems—each system responsible for a particular function of the body.

These systems include :—

The "Maintenance" Systems shown in the diagram. These keep the cells in perfect condition however much the environment outside the body may change. Most of the maintenance of the cells is performed by means of a special fluid, *blood,* which is carried in tubes, *blood vessels,* to all parts of the body. Blood is able to transfer many substances to or from each cell.

The Skeleton, which comprises:—
1. The supporting and protective framework of bone and cartilage.

2. The joints linking the bones.

The Muscles controlling the movements at the joints.

The Skin which encloses and protects the body and is important for the regulation of its temperature.

The Nervous System, which co-ordinates the activities of the different parts of the body.

The Reproductive System, which is described in the third section of this book.

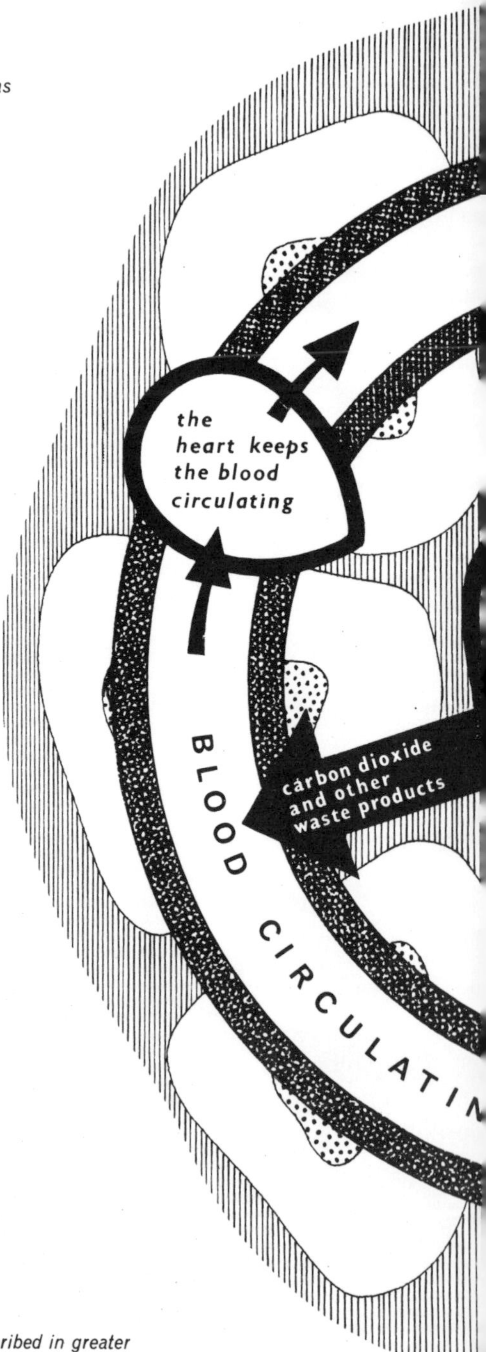

In the following pages the systems of the body are described in greater detail.

the
heart keeps
the blood
circulating

BLOOD

carbon dioxide
and other
waste products

CIRCULATIN

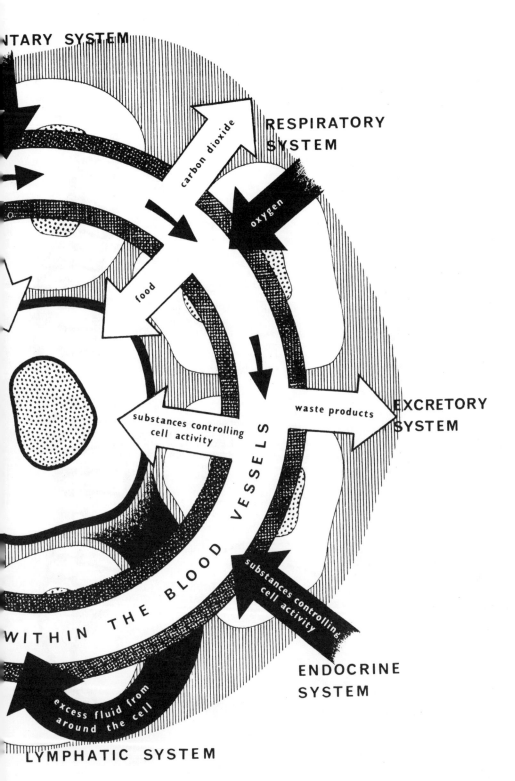

the skeleton

Most tissues are soft and easily damaged. The *skeleton*, made of bone and cartilage, gives support and protection, and also provides a rigid attachment for the muscles.

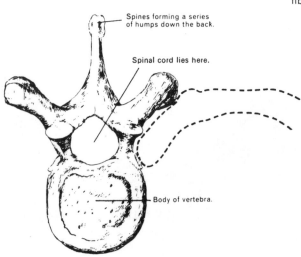

The skull protects the brain and the orbits protect the eyeballs.

The spine is a strut to support the trunk and a bony tube to protect the spinal cord.

The spine is made up of a series of bony blocks – the *vertebrae*.

Each vertebral body is joined to the one below by a thick *disc* made of fibrocartilage.

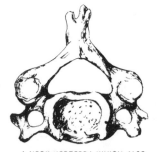

A NECK VERTEBRA WHICH ALSO PROTECTS TWO LARGE BLOOD VESSELS RUNNING UP TO THE BRAIN.

Spines forming a series of humps down the back.

Spinal cord lies here.

Body of vertebra.

A TYPICAL VERTEBRA.

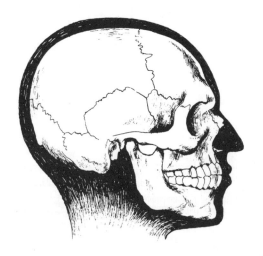

the skull

The bony skull is made up of many bones fitting together.

Some of the skull bones, especially those above and below the orbit, contain air filled spaces – the *sinuses*.

The upper and lower jaws provide rigid attachments for teeth

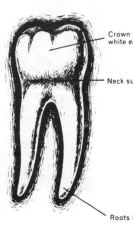

Crown covered by hard white *enamel*.

Neck surrounded by gum.

Roots in the jaw bone.

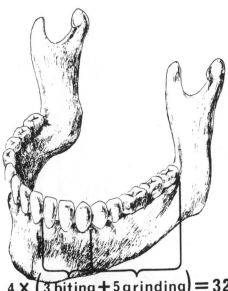

total teeth $4 \times \left(3 \text{ biting} + 5 \text{ grinding} \right) = 32$

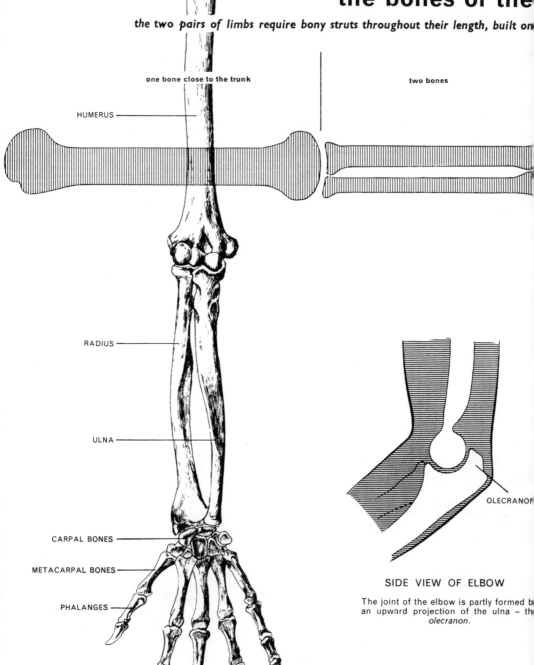

the bones of the

the two pairs of limbs require bony struts throughout their length, built on

one bone close to the trunk

two bones

HUMERUS

RADIUS

ULNA

CARPAL BONES

METACARPAL BONES

PHALANGES

OLECRANON

SIDE VIEW OF ELBOW

The joint of the elbow is partly formed by
an upward projection of the ulna – the
olecranon.

limbs

standard pattern.

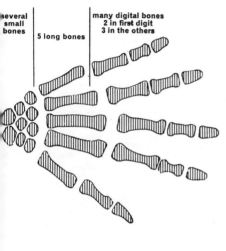

several
small
bones

5 long bones

many digital bones
2 in first digit
3 in the others

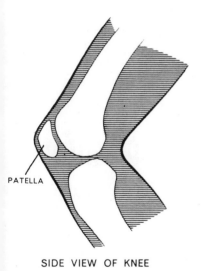

PATELLA

SIDE VIEW OF KNEE

The knee cap *(patella)* is a separate bone
in front of the *paired* condyles of the femur.

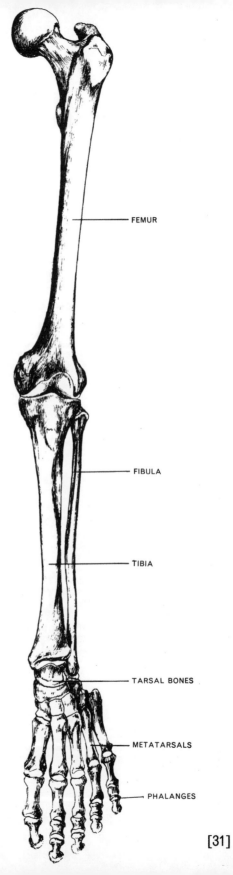

FEMUR

FIBULA

TIBIA

TARSAL BONES

METATARSALS

PHALANGES

[31]

the chest (thorax)

The thoracic cage protects vital
organs within the chest,
especially the heart and lungs.
Some of the upper abdominal
organs are also sheltered within
it.

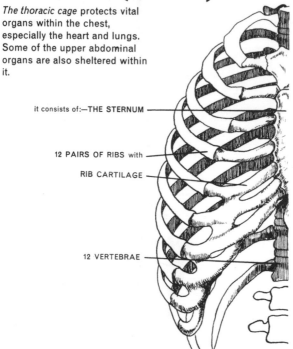
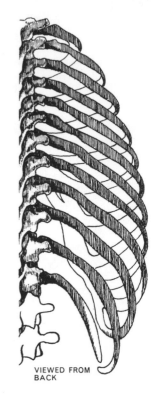

it consists of:—THE STERNUM

12 PAIRS OF RIBS with

RIB CARTILAGE

12 VERTEBRAE

VIEWED
FROM FRONT

VIEWED FROM
BACK

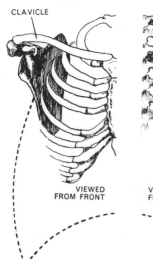

CLAVICLE

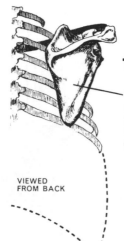

the shoulder girdle

The shoulder blade (SCAPULA)
slides over the back and side of
the ribs. It is joined to the breast
bone by the collar bone
(CLAVICLE).

VIEWED
FROM FRONT

VIEWED
FROM BACK

the abdomen

Apart from the spine running down the
back there are no bones within the
abdominal wall. But the lower abdominal
organs are surrounded by the flat bones
of the pelvic girdle.

the pelvic girdle

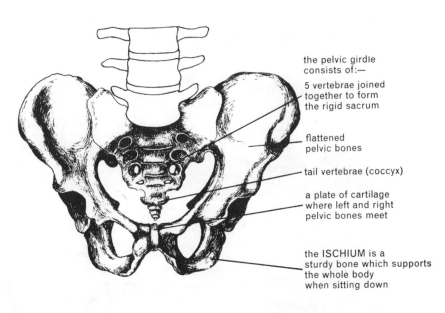

the pelvic girdle
consists of:—

5 vertebrae joined
together to form
the rigid sacrum

flattened
pelvic bones

tail vertebrae (coccyx)

a plate of cartilage
where left and right
pelvic bones meet

the ISCHIUM is a
sturdy bone which supports
the whole body
when sitting down

The junctions between neighbouring bones constitute the joints

The
freely movable
joints *the synovial joints*

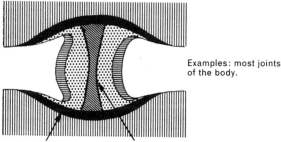

Examples: most joints of the body.

Usually there are thick bands of white fibres – the *ligaments* – assisting the *capsule*.

In a few joints there is a disc of fibro-cartilage here with a synovial cavity on each side.

the
less movable
joints *the cartilaginous joints*

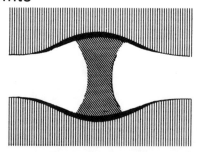

The *vertebrae* are linked mainly by cartilaginous joints between the vertebral bodies.

These "discs" act as shock absorbers as well as allowing one *vertebra* to tilt or rotate on the next.

the fibrous joints

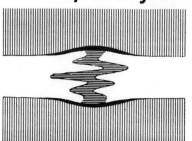

The bones of the skull are united by *fibrous joints* that allow no movement at all.

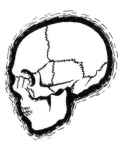

particular joints

Movements within the body necessitating synovial joints include:—

1. Opening and closing the jaws as in chewing or speaking.

2. Movements between the bones of the limbs as in walking.

3. Moving the ribs in breathing.

Synovial joints are of several types.

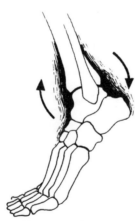

At the shoulder and hip there are *ball-and-socket* joints allowing the limb to swing and turn (rotate) in all directions.

The ankle joints are *hinge joints* allowing bending and straightening only.

The radius and ulna are linked by *pivot joints* allowing the forearm to rotate so that the palm can face the sky or the ground.

THE OUTER FEMORAL CONDYLE FITS HERE.

THE INNER FEMORAL CONDYLE FITS HERE.

The Knee is not a perfect hinge because some rotation can occur as well as bending and straightening. It contains two C-shaped pieces of fibrocartilage, often referred to as the "cartilages" of the knee.

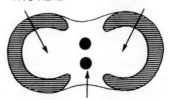

VIEW OF THE TOP OF THE TIBIA AFTER REMOVAL OF THE FEMUR.

Two stout ligaments pass from here to the femur.

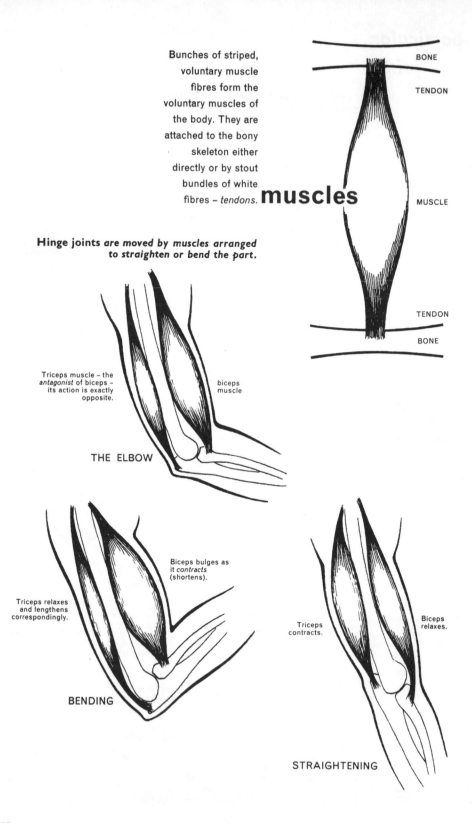

Bunches of striped, voluntary muscle fibres form the voluntary muscles of the body. They are attached to the bony skeleton either directly or by stout bundles of white fibres – *tendons*. **muscles**

BONE

TENDON

MUSCLE

TENDON

BONE

Hinge joints *are moved by muscles arranged to straighten or bend the part.*

Triceps muscle – the *antagonist* of biceps – its action is exactly opposite.

biceps muscle

THE ELBOW

Biceps bulges as it *contracts* (shortens).

Triceps relaxes and lengthens correspondingly.

BENDING

Triceps contracts.

Biceps relaxes.

STRAIGHTENING

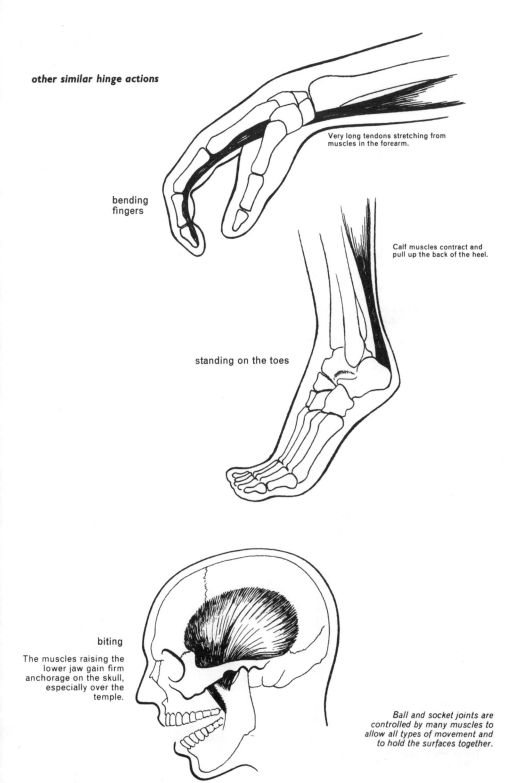

other similar hinge actions

Very long tendons stretching from muscles in the forearm.

bending fingers

Calf muscles contract and pull up the back of the heel.

standing on the toes

biting

The muscles raising the lower jaw gain firm anchorage on the skull, especially over the temple.

Ball and socket joints are controlled by many muscles to allow all types of movement and to hold the surfaces together.

muscles

some well known muscles are :—

at the shoulder

Many large muscles are attached to the
surface of the thoracic cage.

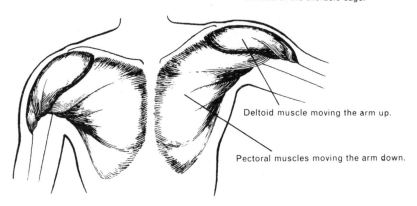

Deltoid muscle moving the arm up.

Pectoral muscles moving the arm down.

at the hip and thigh

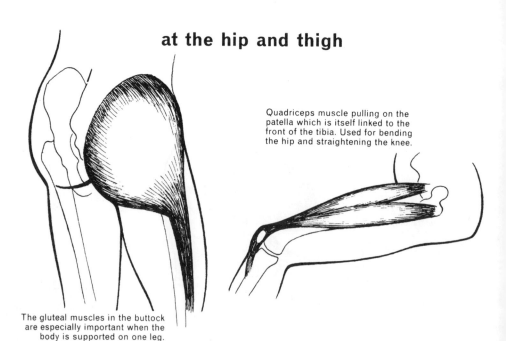

Quadriceps muscle pulling on the
patella which is itself linked to the
front of the tibia. Used for bending
the hip and straightening the knee.

The gluteal muscles in the buttock
are especially important when the
body is supported on one leg.

flat muscles

Certain muscles have their fibres arranged in flattened sheets and their tendons are similarly flattened.

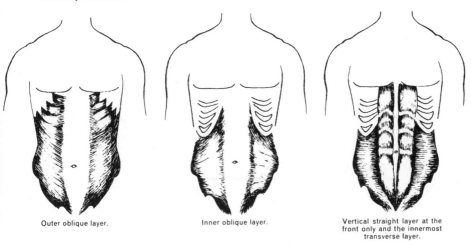

Outer oblique layer.

Inner oblique layer.

Vertical straight layer at the front only and the innermost transverse layer.

The muscles of the abdominal wall are arranged like the layers of 3-ply wood to give the maximum support.

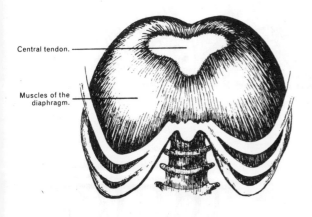

Central tendon.

Muscles of the diaphragm.

The muscle fibres of the diaphragm radiate from the central tendon to be attached to the inner surface of the chest wall. On contraction they pull the tendon down, enlarging the capacity of the chest and compressing the abdominal organs.

the control of
muscular contraction

We can control the activity of every
muscle in the body by means of signals
sent along the nerve fibres from the brain
and spinal cord to the muscles

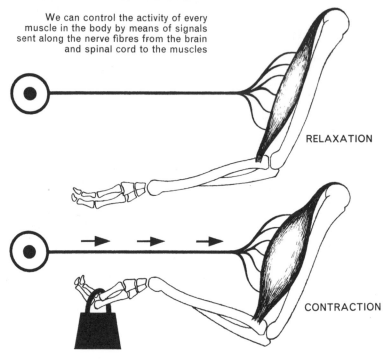

RELAXATION

CONTRACTION

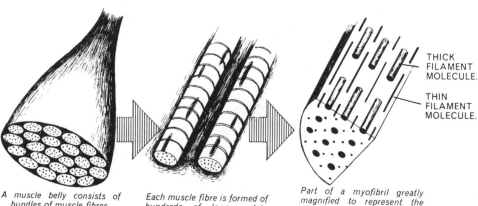

THICK
FILAMENT
MOLECULE.

THIN
FILAMENT
MOLECULE.

*A muscle belly consists of
bundles of muscle fibres.*

*Each muscle fibre is formed of
hundreds of long protein
threads – the **myofibrils.***

*Part of a myofibril greatly
magnified to represent the
position of the protein
molecules.*

**The power of muscular contraction results
from the forces exerted by the complex
filamentous molecules when they move
towards each other and overlap. This is
represented diagrammatically above.**

the grading of
muscular contraction

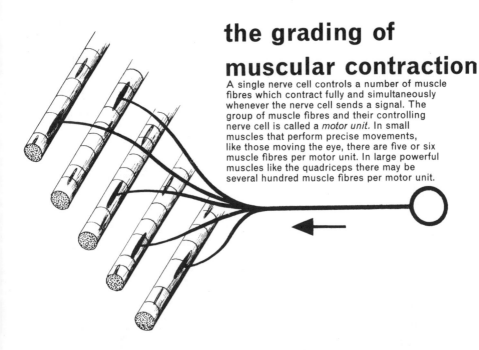

A single nerve cell controls a number of muscle fibres which contract fully and simultaneously whenever the nerve cell sends a signal. The group of muscle fibres and their controlling nerve cell is called a *motor unit*. In small muscles that perform precise movements, like those moving the eye, there are five or six muscle fibres per motor unit. In large powerful muscles like the quadriceps there may be several hundred muscle fibres per motor unit.

The smallest contraction is the response of a single motor unit.

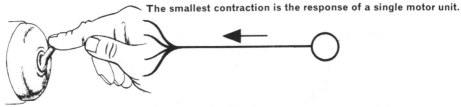

The strongest contraction is the response of all the units.

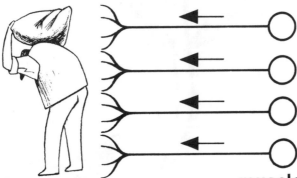

muscle energy

The energy for muscular contraction comes from the breakdown of the glycogen which is stored in all muscles. Large quantities of oxygen have to be delivered by the blood and large amounts of waste products – acids and carbon dioxide – have to be removed. In severe exercise the muscle cannot get enough oxygen but this "oxygen debt" can be repaid later and the oxygen-starved muscle can go on contracting effectively for a time.

The nervous system enables the body to react to internal and external changes. The reaction or *response* to the change may be automatic (involuntary) or under the control of the will (voluntary).

the nervous

The simplest response is a single involuntary movement, often protective in function.

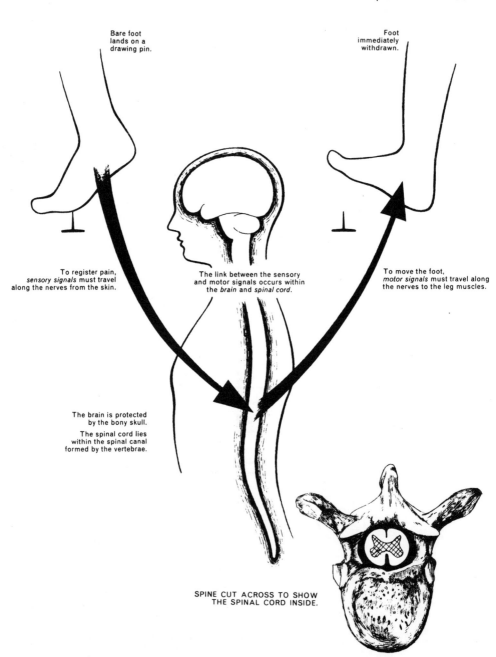

Bare foot lands on a drawing pin.

Foot immediately withdrawn.

To register pain, *sensory signals* must travel along the nerves from the skin.

The link between the sensory and motor signals occurs within the *brain* and *spinal cord*.

To move the foot, *motor signals* must travel along the nerves to the leg muscles.

The brain is protected by the bony skull.

The spinal cord lies within the spinal canal formed by the vertebrae.

SPINE CUT ACROSS TO SHOW THE SPINAL CORD INSIDE.

system

Anything able to set off a sensory signal is called a **stimulus**

Examples of stimuli are:—

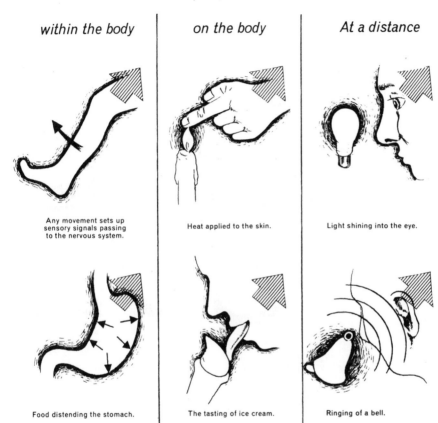

within the body	*on the body*	*At a distance*
Any movement sets up sensory signals passing to the nervous system.	Heat applied to the skin.	Light shining into the eye.
Food distending the stomach.	The tasting of ice cream.	Ringing of a bell.

To be able to respond effectively to stimuli, the nervous system must be able to conduct signals very rapidly. Its cell unit, the **neurone,** *has this special property of rapid conduction, always in the same direction.*

PECIAL TYPE OF NEURONE WITH
WO AXONS BOTH OF WHICH CONDUCT
ENSORY SIGNALS AS IN THE FIRST
ART OF THE REFLEX ARC.

COMMON TYPE OF NEURONE WITH SEVERAL *DENDRITES*
LEADING TO THE CELL BODY AND ONE *AXON* LEAVING IT.

automatic responses

reflexes

If a stimulus reaches the skin
a sensory signal passes into
the back of the spinal cord.

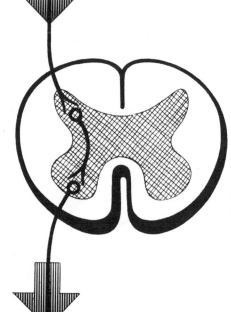

Here a second neurone
conducts the signal to the
dendrites of a third, *final
neurone,* whose axon leaves
the front of the spinal cord
and runs to a muscle.

The cell bodies and
dendrites of the spinal
cord are collected in a
central H-shaped
column of *grey matter.*
The outer rim of *white*
matter consists of
bundles of axons called
tracts which run up to
the brain or descend
from it. Each axon
usually has a fatty
insulating sheath.

The muscle then causes a
movement of part of the body.

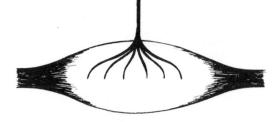

An immediate, involuntary response to a stimulus – for
example, pulling away from a sharp object or blinking –
is called a *reflex.* The pathway for the nervous signals
involved is a *reflex arc* and forms an essential part of the
basic design of the body.

postural reflexes

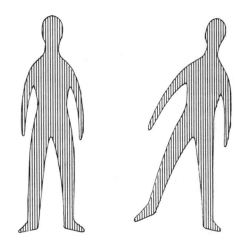

Any movement of one part of the body involves automatic adjustments of other parts which are carried out by means of *postural reflexes*.

For example, if the right leg is lifted off the ground the body must be tilted to the left to maintain the balance.

conditioned reflexes

If the body relied on simple reflexes only, a certain response would always be associated with the same stimulus. In practice, many reflexes can be modified so that a particular response can be evoked by different stimuli. This is well demonstrated by some famous experiments carried out on dogs.

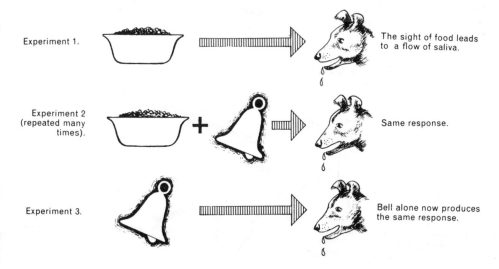

Experiment 1.

The sight of food leads to a flow of saliva.

Experiment 2 (repeated many times).

Same response.

Experiment 3.

Bell alone now produces the same response.

The new reflex which has been set up is called a *conditioned reflex*. This process is an important factor in learning by experience.

sensory functions

All sensory signals entering the spinal cord, besides often setting off reflex responses, are conducted along ascending tracts to the brain. Most of the signals cross to the opposite side of the brain and link up with a third series of neurones located in a large body called the *thalamus*. Many of the remainder end in the *cerebellum* on the same side of the body.

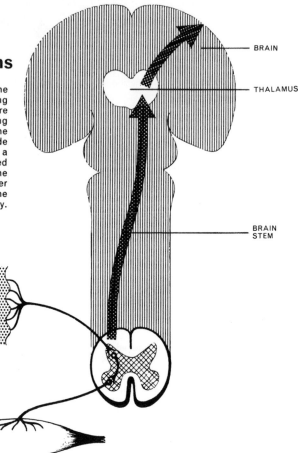

BRAIN

THALAMUS

BRAIN STEM

the sensory areas of the brain

The brain has three main parts – the *cerebrum*, *cerebellum* and *brain stem*.

Most of the cell bodies of the neurones are concentrated at the surface of the cerebrum. The signals they receive from many sources are continually being linked together to build up a pattern of the various stimuli affecting the body at any moment. We are not conscious of the whole of the pattern at any given time, but we can direct our attention to any part of it at will.

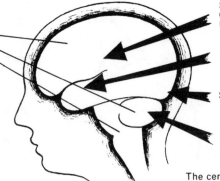

SIGNALS FROM THE SKIN OF THE FACE, TRUNK AND LIMBS.

SIGNALS FROM THE EARS.

SIGNALS FROM THE EYES.

SIGNALS CONCERNING POSTURE AND BALANCE.

The cerebrum is divided into two halves – the *cerebral hemispheres*. Each half deals mainly with signals from stimuli affecting the opposite side of the body.

of the brain

motor functions

The final neurone of a spinal reflex arc can receive signals from the brain, especially from the opposite side. These may be added to the reflex signals but often they have the opposite effect and prevent reflex signals from continuing to the muscles.

For example, a waiter who knowingly picks up a very hot plate will not drop it because a signal from the brain blocks the reflex that would otherwise lead to the automatic release of a painful object.

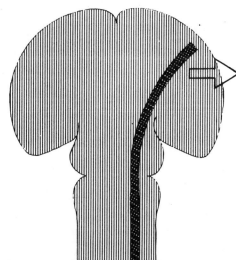

Motor signals from the brain pass to the muscles of the head causing movement of the eyes, tongue, jaws, etc.

the motor areas of the brain

Neurones here produce voluntary movements of face trunk and limbs

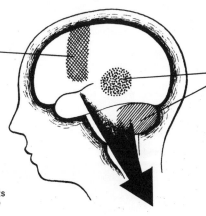

Neurones near the centre of each cerebral hemisphere and within the cerebellum are responsible for the organisation of the complicated muscular activity that is needed for various postural movements—such as swinging the arms when walking—and for accurate balance.

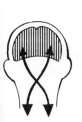

Each cerebral hemisphere is responsible for the voluntary movements of the opposite side of the body.

other functions of the brain

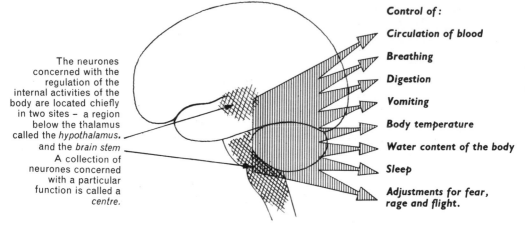

The neurones concerned with the regulation of the internal activities of the body are located chiefly in two sites – a region below the thalamus called the *hypothalamus*, and the *brain stem* A collection of neurones concerned with a particular function is called a *centre*.

Control of:

Circulation of blood

Breathing

Digestion

Vomiting

Body temperature

Water content of the body

Sleep

Adjustments for fear, rage and flight.

The detailed control of these functions is carried out by means of the **Autonomic Nervous System** *(page 50).*

Higher functions such as thought and memory are attributes of the brain as a whole rather than of any particular part. However, the study of disordered brains suggests that certain areas are especially important.

Self-control and co-operative, socially desirable behaviour.

Control and understanding of speech, situated in the left cerebral hemisphere only, in right handed people.

MEMORY

The functions that are disturbed if these areas of the cerebrum are diseased or injured.

The axons outside the brain and spinal cord are arranged in bundles called *nerves*. The individual axons are usually covered by fatty insulating sheaths and always have an outer cover of protoplasm. Nerves usually contain some axons transmitting sensory signals and some transmitting motor signals.

nerves

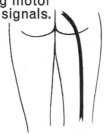

Sciatic nerve in the buttock and back of thigh carrying signals to and from the leg and foot.

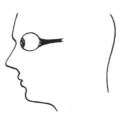

Optic nerve running from the eye to the brain.

Trigeminal nerve carrying sensory signals from the skin of the face and motor signals to the muscles moving the lower jaw.

coverings of the central nervous system

The very delicate brain and spinal cord are well protected.

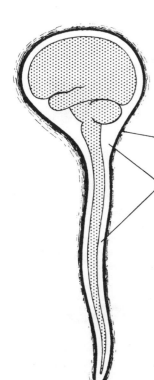

Thick membrane lined by two thin delicate ones.

Watery fluid acting as a water bath or cushion around the brain and spinal cord – *cerebrospinal fluid*.

cerebrospinal fluid

The fluid is formed within cavities, called *ventricles*, inside the brain, by being filtered out of the blood. It passes out into a space around the central nervous system through holes at the back of the brain stem. It is finally absorbed by the veins lining the skull.

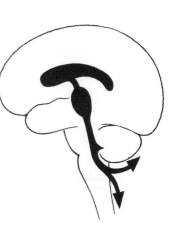

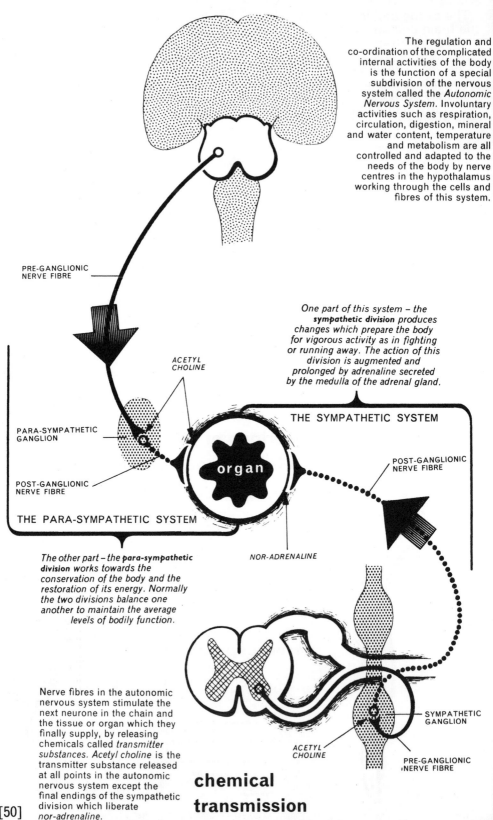

The regulation and co-ordination of the complicated internal activities of the body is the function of a special subdivision of the nervous system called the *Autonomic Nervous System.* Involuntary activities such as respiration, circulation, digestion, mineral and water content, temperature and metabolism are all controlled and adapted to the needs of the body by nerve centres in the hypothalamus working through the cells and fibres of this system.

PRE-GANGLIONIC
NERVE FIBRE

One part of this system – the **sympathetic division** produces changes which prepare the body for vigorous activity as in fighting or running away. The action of this division is augmented and prolonged by adrenaline secreted by the medulla of the adrenal gland.

ACETYL
CHOLINE

THE SYMPATHETIC SYSTEM

PARA-SYMPATHETIC
GANGLION

organ

POST-GANGLIONIC
NERVE FIBRE

POST-GANGLIONIC
NERVE FIBRE

THE PARA-SYMPATHETIC SYSTEM

NOR-ADRENALINE

The other part – the **para-sympathetic division** works towards the conservation of the body and the restoration of its energy. Normally the two divisions balance one another to maintain the average levels of bodily function.

SYMPATHETIC
GANGLION

Nerve fibres in the autonomic nervous system stimulate the next neurone in the chain and the tissue or organ which they finally supply, by releasing chemicals called *transmitter substances. Acetyl choline* is the transmitter substance released at all points in the autonomic nervous system except the final endings of the sympathetic division which liberate *nor-adrenaline.*

ACETYL
CHOLINE

PRE-GANGLIONIC
NERVE FIBRE

**chemical
transmission**

autonomic nervous system

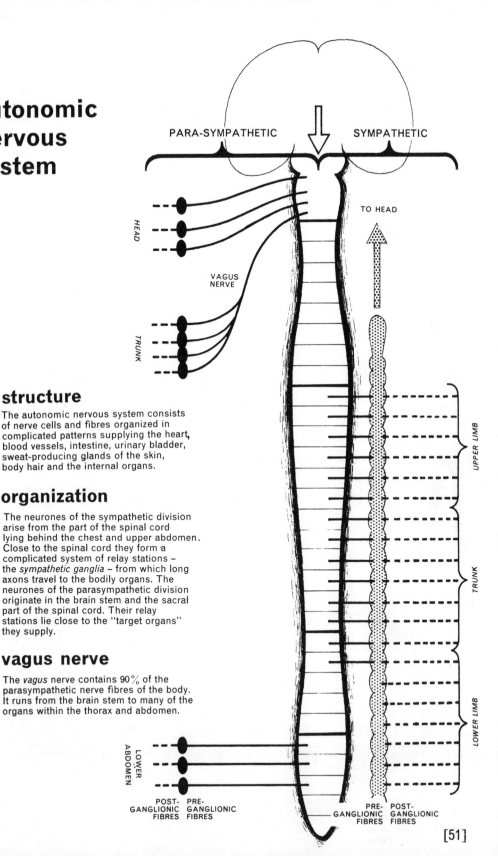

PARA-SYMPATHETIC

SYMPATHETIC

HEAD

TO HEAD

VAGUS NERVE

TRUNK

structure

The autonomic nervous system consists of nerve cells and fibres organized in complicated patterns supplying the heart, blood vessels, intestine, urinary bladder, sweat-producing glands of the skin, body hair and the internal organs.

organization

The neurones of the sympathetic division arise from the part of the spinal cord lying behind the chest and upper abdomen. Close to the spinal cord they form a complicated system of relay stations – the *sympathetic ganglia* – from which long axons travel to the bodily organs. The neurones of the parasympathetic division originate in the brain stem and the sacral part of the spinal cord. Their relay stations lie close to the "target organs" they supply.

vagus nerve

The *vagus* nerve contains 90% of the parasympathetic nerve fibres of the body. It runs from the brain stem to many of the organs within the thorax and abdomen.

UPPER LIMB

TRUNK

LOWER LIMB

LOWER ABDOMEN

POST-GANGLIONIC FIBRES

PRE-GANGLIONIC FIBRES

PRE-GANGLIONIC FIBRES

POST-GANGLIONIC FIBRES

[51]

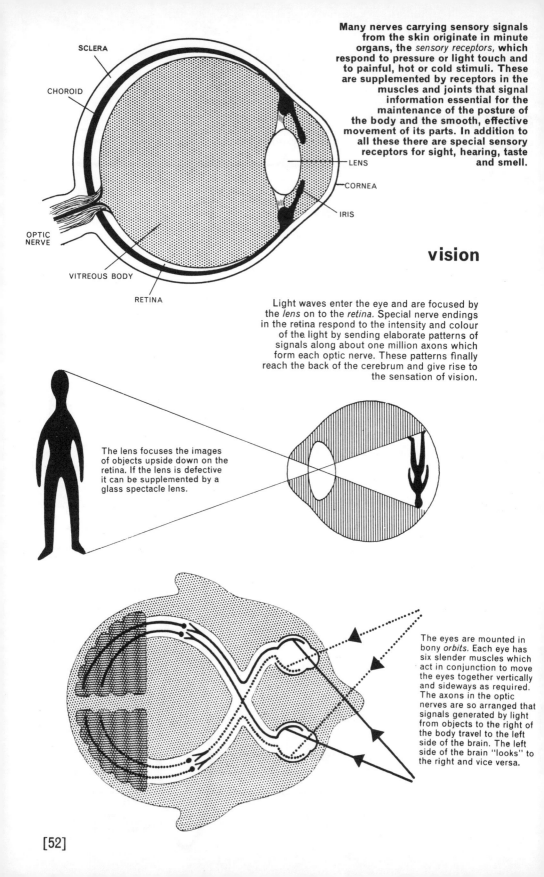

SCLERA

CHOROID

Many nerves carrying sensory signals from the skin originate in minute organs, the *sensory receptors*, which respond to pressure or light touch and to painful, hot or cold stimuli. These are supplemented by receptors in the muscles and joints that signal information essential for the maintenance of the posture of the body and the smooth, effective movement of its parts. In addition to all these there are special sensory receptors for sight, hearing, taste and smell.

LENS

CORNEA

IRIS

vision

OPTIC NERVE

VITREOUS BODY

RETINA

Light waves enter the eye and are focused by the *lens* on to the *retina*. Special nerve endings in the retina respond to the intensity and colour of the light by sending elaborate patterns of signals along about one million axons which form each optic nerve. These patterns finally reach the back of the cerebrum and give rise to the sensation of vision.

The lens focuses the images of objects upside down on the retina. If the lens is defective it can be supplemented by a glass spectacle lens.

The eyes are mounted in bony *orbits*. Each eye has six slender muscles which act in conjunction to move the eyes together vertically and sideways as required. The axons in the optic nerves are so arranged that signals generated by light from objects to the right of the body travel to the left side of the brain. The left side of the brain "looks" to the right and vice versa.

special senses

hearing

Sound waves are channelled by the outer ear to a "membrane drum" which vibrates. The vibrations are transmitted by tiny levers of bone to a fluid-filled spiral organ containing sensory receptors, that are sensitive to vibration. Signals from them are carried by axons in the *auditory nerve* to the brain stem and finally to the cerebral hemisphere (page 46). The fluid also exends into three semi-circular canals in each ear which are set at right angles to each other. They behave like tiny spirit levels and special receptors in their walls signal changes of position of the head in space. These sensory signals are essential to proper balance and posture.

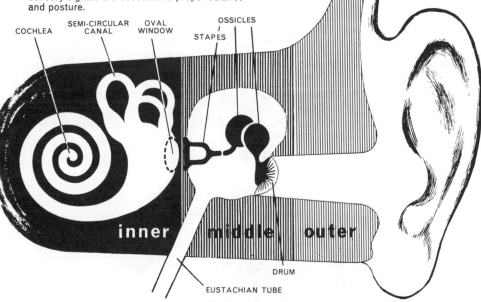

The Eustachian tube connects the middle ear to a cavity behind the nose and serves to balance the air pressure between the outer and middle ears. Swallowing opens the Eustachian tube momentarily and prevents discomfort or injury when the air pressure is changing rapidly as in an aircraft descent.

taste and smell

Special receptors in the tongue, palate and upper nose respond to chemical compounds in food, drink and the air. The resulting signals finally give rise to the sensations of taste and smell. The smell receptors can detect as little as one millionth of a milligram of some substances. (A milligram is one thousandth of a gram, which is itself about one thirtieth of an ounce.)

respiratory

Respiration means the transfer of oxygen from the air to the tissues of the body and the transfer of carbon dioxide from the tissues to the outside air.

The outside air which contains the essential gas, oxygen, never comes into direct contact with the bulk of the cells of the body. A system of branching tubes is therefore necessary to admit air to the interior of the body and to allow the discharge of the waste gas, carbon dioxide.

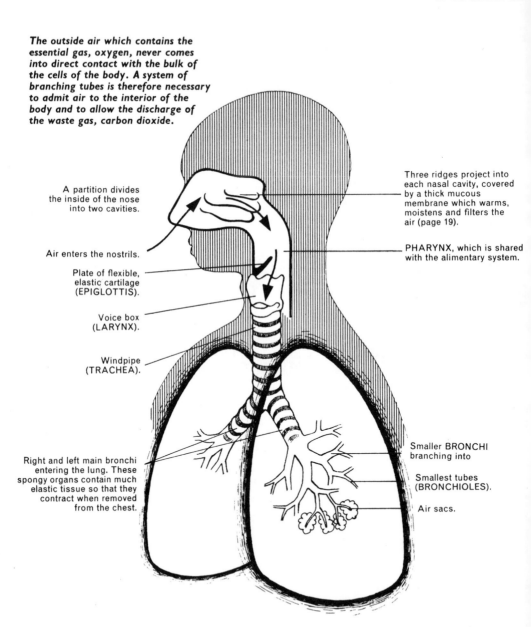

A partition divides the inside of the nose into two cavities.

Air enters the nostrils.

Plate of flexible, elastic cartilage (EPIGLOTTIS).

Voice box (LARYNX).

Windpipe (TRACHEA).

Right and left main bronchi entering the lung. These spongy organs contain much elastic tissue so that they contract when removed from the chest.

Three ridges project into each nasal cavity, covered by a thick mucous membrane which warms, moistens and filters the air (page 19).

PHARYNX, which is shared with the alimentary system.

Smaller BRONCHI branching into

Smallest tubes (BRONCHIOLES).

Air sacs.

system

Each air sac is in close contact with a network of narrow, thin-walled vessels (capillaries).

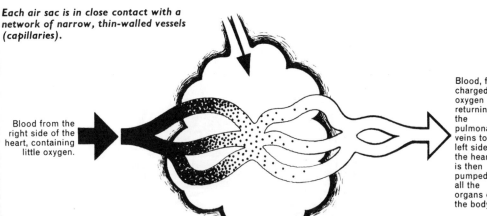

Blood from the right side of the heart, containing little oxygen.

Blood, fully charged with oxygen returning in the pulmonary veins to the left side of the heart. It is then pumped to all the organs of the body.

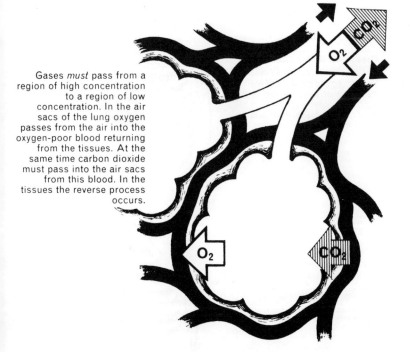

Gases *must* pass from a region of high concentration to a region of low concentration. In the air sacs of the lung oxygen passes from the air into the oxygen-poor blood returning from the tissues. At the same time carbon dioxide must pass into the air sacs from this blood. In the tissues the reverse process occurs.

O_2

CO_2

O_2

CO_2

the pleural cavities

can best be understood by considering what happens when a hole is made in the wall of the chest.

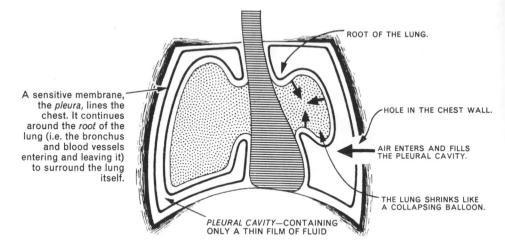

ROOT OF THE LUNG.

A sensitive membrane, the *pleura*, lines the chest. It continues around the *root* of the lung (i.e. the bronchus and blood vessels entering and leaving it) to surround the lung itself.

HOLE IN THE CHEST WALL.

AIR ENTERS AND FILLS THE PLEURAL CAVITY.

THE LUNG SHRINKS LIKE A COLLAPSING BALLOON.

PLEURAL CAVITY—CONTAINING ONLY A THIN FILM OF FLUID

movements of respiration

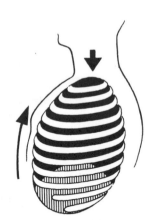

Breathing in (inspiration).
Air is actively drawn into the lungs by enlarging the capacity of the chest. The ribs are elevated by muscles attached to them. The muscle of the diaphragm contracts and it becomes less domed.

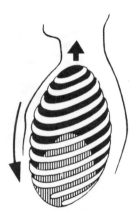

Breathing out (expiration).
This is usually done merely by relaxing the muscles of the ribs and diaphragm. The ribs return to their former positions and the diaphragm rises, all aided by the elastic contraction of the lungs.

system

control of respiration

The main control is exerted by the
amount of carbon dioxide in the
blood circulating through the
respiratory centre in the brain stem.
Excess carbon dioxide stimulates
the respiratory centre to send out
nerve signals which increase the
rate and depth of respiration.
Carbon dioxide is "washed out"
of the blood into the lungs. The
blood level therefore falls and
respiration eases off. If this goes
too far carbon dioxide is retained
to excess in the blood and again
stimulates the respiratory centre.
In health this control is extremely
accurate and precise.

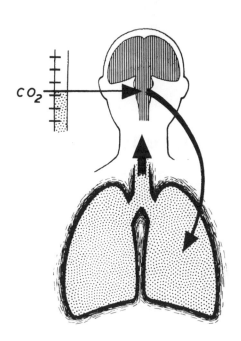

the larynx

Air passing up the trachea has to pass between two folds –
the vocal cords – stretched across the larynx. These
cords vibrate and produce sounds. They can be adjusted
as follows:—

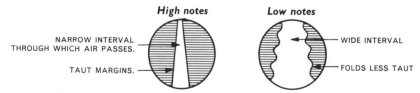

High notes

NARROW INTERVAL
THROUGH WHICH AIR PASSES.

TAUT MARGINS.

Low notes

WIDE INTERVAL

FOLDS LESS TAUT

View into the larynx from above.

the pharynx

is the cavity lying behind the nose, the mouth and the upper part
of the larynx. It is shared with the alimentary system but food
rarely passes into the trachea because the soft palate, epiglottis
and larynx all move to prevent this accident.

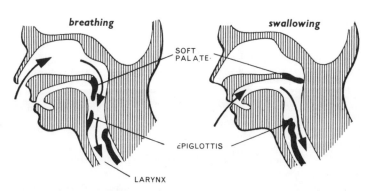

breathing

swallowing

SOFT
PALATE

EPIGLOTTIS

LARYNX

[57]

the alimentary system

This is the system which converts *food* into substances that the body cells can use as sources of *energy*. It consists essentially of a long twisted tube leading from the mouth to the anus.

general functions

Layers of unstriped muscle which contract and push the contents forward.

Mucous membrane lined by columnar cells.

The surface area of mucous membrane is extremely large :—

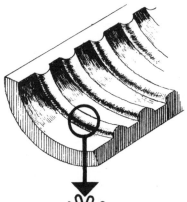

When split open large numbers of circular *FOLDS* are seen.

FOLD

In many parts there are fine finger-like projections; each is called a VILLUS.

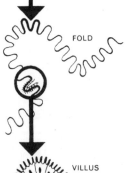

VILLUS

Each villus is clothed with columnar cells which have extremely small brush-like projections.

functions of the alimentary system

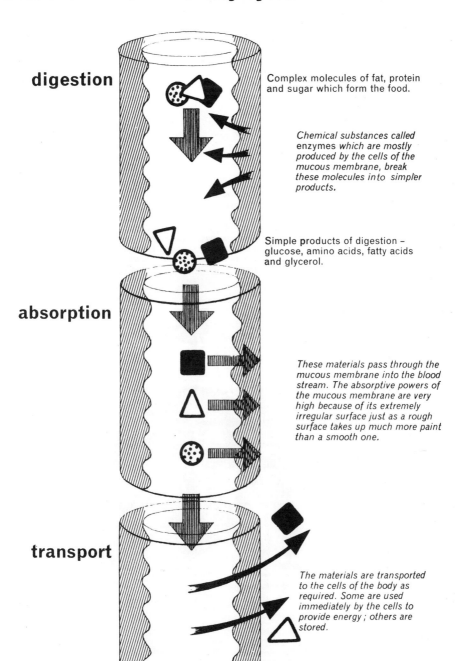

digestion

Complex molecules of fat, protein and sugar which form the food.

Chemical substances called enzymes which are mostly produced by the cells of the mucous membrane, break these molecules into simpler products.

Simple products of digestion – glucose, amino acids, fatty acids and glycerol.

absorption

These materials pass through the mucous membrane into the blood stream. The absorptive powers of the mucous membrane are very high because of its extremely irregular surface just as a rough surface takes up much more paint than a smooth one.

transport

The materials are transported to the cells of the body as required. Some are used immediately by the cells to provide energy ; others are stored.

the alimentary system   (cont.)

mastication and swallowing

Within the mouth the food is cut and ground by the *teeth* and moistened by the *saliva*. Saliva is a sticky, lubricating fluid containing an enzyme, *ptyalin*, which acts on starch. It is produced by three pairs of special *salivary glands – parotid, submandibular* and *sublingual*. The softened food is thrust back by the *tongue* beyond the *palate* into a funnel shaped cavity – the *pharynx* (page 57).

The inside of the mouth can readily be studied with the aid of a mirror. Look for all the features indicated.

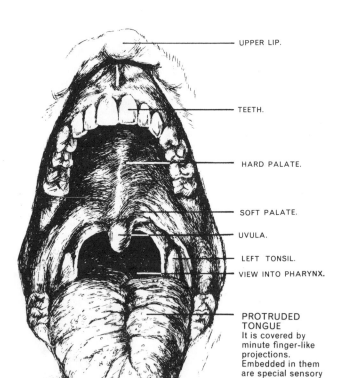

UPPER LIP.

TEETH.

HARD PALATE.

SOFT PALATE.

UVULA.

LEFT TONSIL.

VIEW INTO PHARYNX.

PROTRUDED TONGUE
It is covered by minute finger-like projections. Embedded in them are special sensory receptors – *taste buds* – which are sensitive to sweet, salt, sour and bitter tastes. The subtleties of flavour depend largely on the sense of smell.

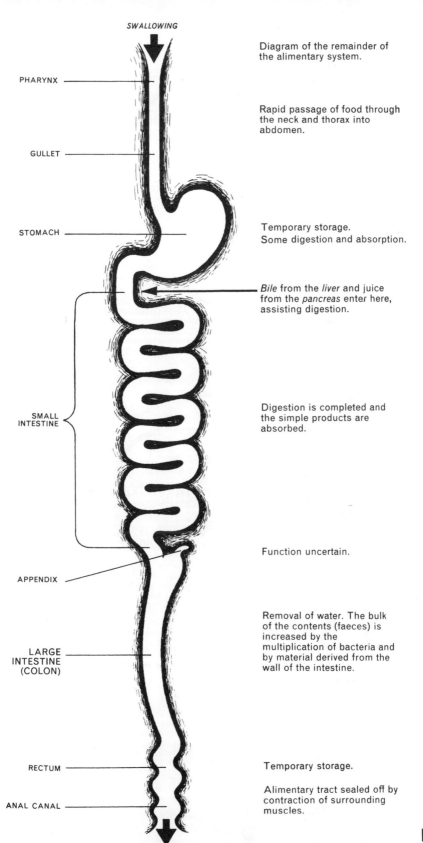

SWALLOWING

Diagram of the remainder of the alimentary system.

PHARYNX

Rapid passage of food through the neck and thorax into abdomen.

GULLET

STOMACH

Temporary storage.
Some digestion and absorption.

Bile from the *liver* and juice from the *pancreas* enter here, assisting digestion.

SMALL INTESTINE

Digestion is completed and the simple products are absorbed.

Function uncertain.

APPENDIX

LARGE INTESTINE (COLON)

Removal of water. The bulk of the contents (faeces) is increased by the multiplication of bacteria and by material derived from the wall of the intestine.

RECTUM

Temporary storage.

ANAL CANAL

Alimentary tract sealed off by contraction of surrounding muscles.

DEFAECATION

[61]

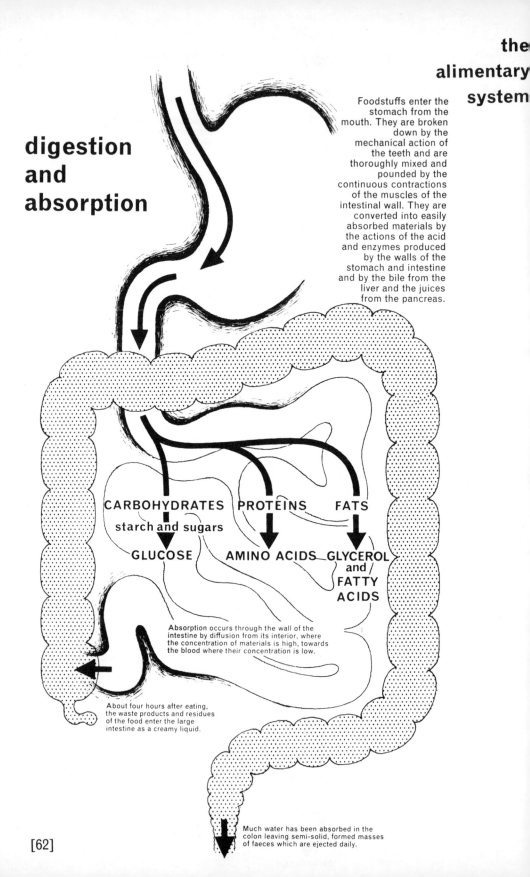

digestion
and
absorption

Foodstuffs enter the stomach from the mouth. They are broken down by the mechanical action of the teeth and are thoroughly mixed and pounded by the continuous contractions of the muscles of the intestinal wall. They are converted into easily absorbed materials by the actions of the acid and enzymes produced by the walls of the stomach and intestine and by the bile from the liver and the juices from the pancreas.

CARBOHYDRATES   PROTEINS   FATS

starch and sugars

GLUCOSE   AMINO ACIDS   GLYCEROL
and
FATTY
ACIDS

Absorption occurs through the wall of the intestine by diffusion from its interior, where the concentration of materials is high, towards the blood where their concentration is low.

About four hours after eating, the waste products and residues of the food enter the large intestine as a creamy liquid.

Much water has been absorbed in the colon leaving semi-solid, formed masses of faeces which are ejected daily.

liver and pancreas

These organs produce respectively *bile* and *pancreatic juice*, which enter the first part of the small intestine – the *duodenum* – and help in the digestion of the food.

the gall bladder

The *gall bladder* – stores and concentrates the bile before use.

functions of bile

1. Breaks fat into globules small enough to be acted upon by enzymes and absorbed easily. 2. Rids the body of substances derived from worn out red blood corpuscles.

functions of pancreatic juice

Pancreatic cells pour the juice into a large duct running the length of the organ and ending in the duodenum. It helps to neutralise the acid from the stomach and supplies enzymes for the further digestion of protein *(trypsin)*, carbohydrate *(amylase)* and fat *(lipase)*.

Both organs have additional functions. The liver is an important food store and some cells in the pancreas function as endocrine glands by secreting insulin which controls the amount of sugar in the blood.

the heart and blood vessels

general plan of the circulatory system

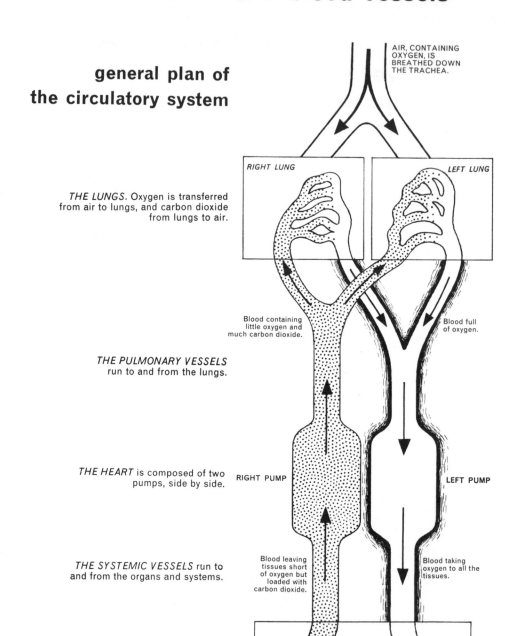

AIR, CONTAINING OXYGEN, IS BREATHED DOWN THE TRACHEA.

RIGHT LUNG

LEFT LUNG

THE LUNGS. Oxygen is transferred from air to lungs, and carbon dioxide from lungs to air.

Blood containing little oxygen and much carbon dioxide.

Blood full of oxygen.

THE PULMONARY VESSELS run to and from the lungs.

RIGHT PUMP

LEFT PUMP

THE HEART is composed of two pumps, side by side.

THE SYSTEMIC VESSELS run to and from the organs and systems.

Blood leaving tissues short of oxygen but loaded with carbon dioxide.

Blood taking oxygen to all the tissues.

THE TISSUES, grouped into systems and organs, take oxygen from the blood and give up carbon dioxide to it. In addition, absorbed food, hormones and waste products pass to and from the tissues and organs in the blood.

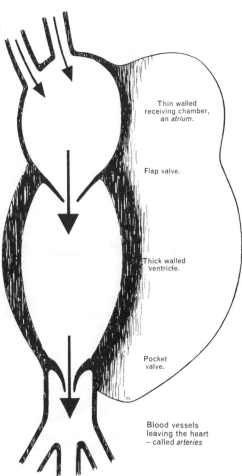

general features
of the heart

Blood vessels entering the heart – called *veins*.

The right and left pumps lie side by side to form a single organ, the *heart,* but they remain independent units. Each pump is made up of two *chambers,* an *atrium* and a *ventricle.* This diagram represents one side of the heart *only.*

The heart and all the blood vessels have a smooth inner surface formed from flattened cells to allow the free flow of blood. The bulk of the heart wall is made of *cardiac muscle* which has the special property of automatic, rhythmic contraction (page 21).

Thin walled receiving chamber, an *atrium.*

Flap valve.

Thick walled ventricle.

Pocket valve.

Blood vessels leaving the heart – called *arteries*

details of types of valves

(1) FLAP VALVE TYPE

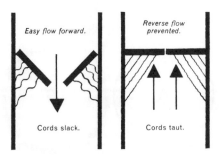

Easy flow forward.

Reverse flow prevented.

Cords slack.

Cords taut.

(2) POCKET VALVE TYPE

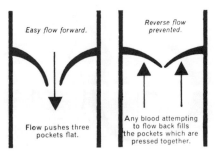

Easy flow forward.

Reverse flow prevented.

Flow pushes three pockets flat.

Any blood attempting to flow back fills the pockets which are pressed together.

arteries

These are the vessels carrying blood from the heart to the tissues and organs. They are of two main types:-

LARGE ARTERIES   The largest coming from the left and right ventricles respectively are called the *aorta* and *pulmonary trunk.* Their walls are mainly *elastic* to help the smooth flow of blood.

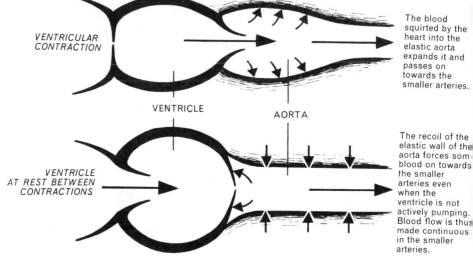

VENTRICULAR
CONTRACTION

VENTRICLE

AORTA

The blood squirted by the heart into the elastic aorta expands it and passes on towards the smaller arteries.

VENTRICLE
AT REST BETWEEN
CONTRACTIONS

The recoil of the elastic wall of the aorta forces some blood on towards the smaller arteries even when the ventricle is not actively pumping. Blood flow is thus made continuous in the smaller arteries.

Even the elastic walls do not smooth the flow completely. The alternating large and small flows produce corresponding phases of high and low pressures within the arteries accounting for the pulse.

SMALL ARTERIES   Not all organs require a maximum supply of oxygen at the same time. The small arteries therefore have plain muscle (page 21) in their walls to reduce the blood flow as required.

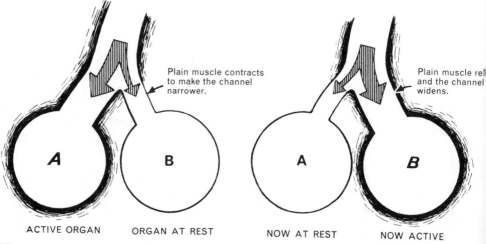

Plain muscle contracts to make the channel narrower.

Plain muscle rel and the channel widens.

A

B

A

B

ACTIVE ORGAN   ORGAN AT REST   NOW AT REST   NOW ACTIVE

the blood vessels

capillaries

The smallest arteries branch eventually into a network of very small vessels called capillaries which run close to all the cells. Their walls are formed by a single layer of flat cells so thin that gases and other chemicals pass easily through them.

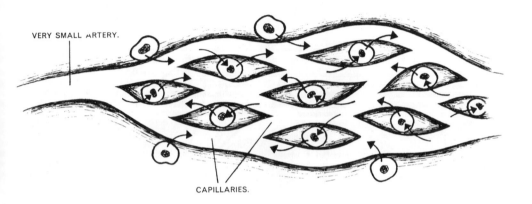

VERY SMALL ARTERY.

CAPILLARIES.

veins

The capillaries rejoin to form small and then increasingly large *VEINS*, returning blood to the heart. Most of the force of the heart beat has been expended in driving the blood thus far, so the pressure within the veins is low. Their walls are composed of layers of white fibres. The space within the veins is relatively large and the walls are thin so that there is little resistance to the flow of blood.

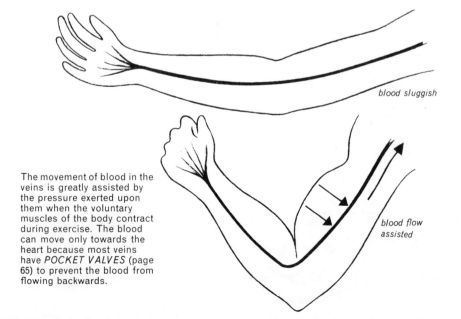

blood sluggish

blood flow assisted

The movement of blood in the veins is greatly assisted by the pressure exerted upon them when the voluntary muscles of the body contract during exercise. The blood can move only towards the heart because most veins have *POCKET VALVES* (page 65) to prevent the blood from flowing backwards.

the structure and function of the heart

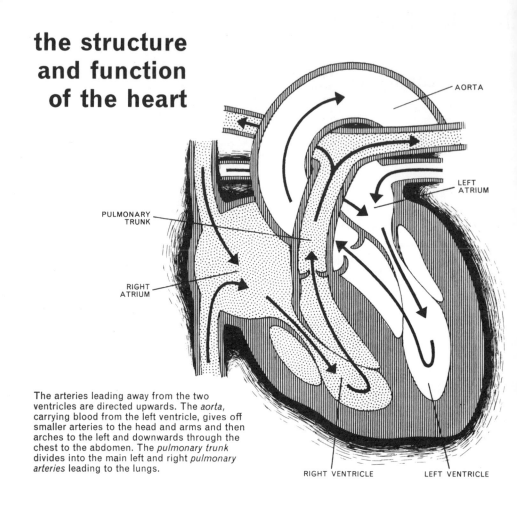

AORTA

LEFT ATRIUM

PULMONARY TRUNK

RIGHT ATRIUM

RIGHT VENTRICLE

LEFT VENTRICLE

The arteries leading away from the two ventricles are directed upwards. The *aorta*, carrying blood from the left ventricle, gives off smaller arteries to the head and arms and then arches to the left and downwards through the chest to the abdomen. The *pulmonary trunk* divides into the main left and right *pulmonary arteries* leading to the lungs.

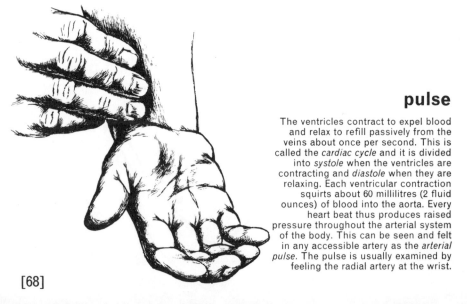

pulse

The ventricles contract to expel blood and relax to refill passively from the veins about once per second. This is called the *cardiac cycle* and it is divided into *systole* when the ventricles are contracting and *diastole* when they are relaxing. Each ventricular contraction squirts about 60 millilitres (2 fluid ounces) of blood into the aorta. Every heart beat thus produces raised pressure throughout the arterial system of the body. This can be seen and felt in any accessible artery as the *arterial pulse*. The pulse is usually examined by feeling the radial artery at the wrist.

the structure and function of blood

Blood is the sticky red fluid inside the blood vessels which carries oxygen and food to the tissues.

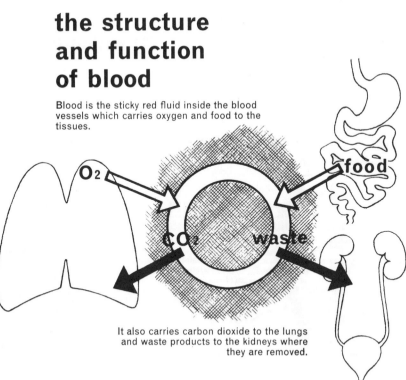

It also carries carbon dioxide to the lungs and waste products to the kidneys where they are removed.

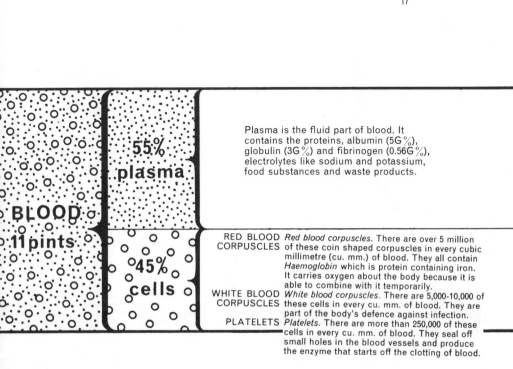

55% plasma

Plasma is the fluid part of blood. It contains the proteins, albumin (5G%), globulin (3G%) and fibrinogen (0.56G%), electrolytes like sodium and potassium, food substances and waste products.

BLOOD 11 pints

45% cells

RED BLOOD CORPUSCLES *Red blood corpuscles.* There are over 5 million of these coin shaped corpuscles in every cubic millimetre (cu. mm.) of blood. They all contain *Haemoglobin* which is protein containing iron. It carries oxygen about the body because it is able to combine with it temporarily.

WHITE BLOOD CORPUSCLES *White blood corpuscles.* There are 5,000-10,000 of these cells in every cu. mm. of blood. They are part of the body's defence against infection.

PLATELETS *Platelets.* There are more than 250,000 of these cells in every cu. mm. of blood. They seal off small holes in the blood vessels and produce the enzyme that starts off the clotting of blood.

(1) within the chest

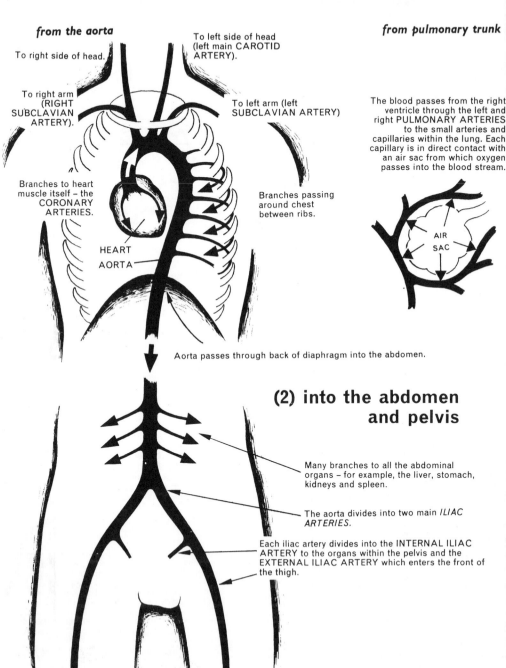

from the aorta

To right side of head.

To left side of head (left main CAROTID ARTERY).

from pulmonary trunk

To right arm (RIGHT SUBCLAVIAN ARTERY).

To left arm (left SUBCLAVIAN ARTERY)

The blood passes from the right ventricle through the left and right PULMONARY ARTERIES to the small arteries and capillaries within the lung. Each capillary is in direct contact with an air sac from which oxygen passes into the blood stream.

Branches to heart muscle itself – the CORONARY ARTERIES.

Branches passing around chest between ribs.

AIR SAC

HEART

AORTA

Aorta passes through back of diaphragm into the abdomen.

(2) into the abdomen and pelvis

Many branches to all the abdominal organs – for example, the liver, stomach, kidneys and spleen.

The aorta divides into two main *ILIAC ARTERIES.*

Each iliac artery divides into the INTERNAL ILIAC ARTERY to the organs within the pelvis and the EXTERNAL ILIAC ARTERY which enters the front of the thigh.

arteries

(3) into the arm

The left SUBCLAVIAN ARTERY passing over the first rib, under the CLAVICLE.

Main BRACHIAL ARTERY divides into two arteries in front of the forearm bones – hence their names

RADIAL ARTERY

ULNAR ARTERY

The two forearm arteries which link up in the palm.

(4) within the head and neck

Each main carotid artery divides into an INTERNAL CAROTID ARTERY, passing to the brain and eye, and an EXTERNAL CAROTID ARTERY, supplying the rest of the head and neck.

The brain is supplied in addition by two VERTEBRAL ARTERIES running in channels within the vertebral column in the neck (page 28).

The four arteries supplying blood to the brain are linked together underneath it by an ARTERIAL CIRCLE, from which arise the branches that enter the brain. Thus the blood supply to the brain need not be interrupted even if one of the main arteries is temporarily blocked.

named arteries (cont.)

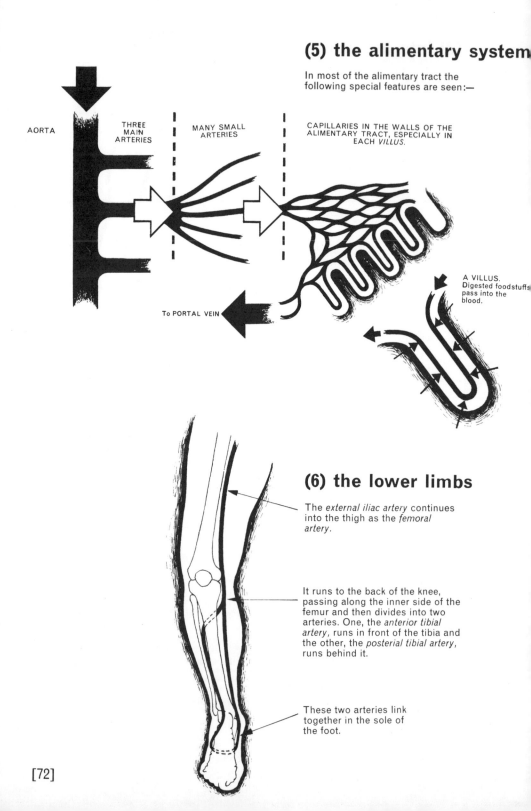

(5) the alimentary system

In most of the alimentary tract the following special features are seen:—

AORTA

THREE MAIN ARTERIES

MANY SMALL ARTERIES

CAPILLARIES IN THE WALLS OF THE ALIMENTARY TRACT, ESPECIALLY IN EACH *VILLUS*.

To PORTAL VEIN

A VILLUS. Digested foodstuffs pass into the blood.

(6) the lower limbs

The *external iliac artery* continues into the thigh as the *femoral artery*.

It runs to the back of the knee, passing along the inner side of the femur and then divides into two arteries. One, the *anterior tibial artery*, runs in front of the tibia and the other, the *posterial tibial artery*, runs behind it.

These two arteries link together in the sole of the foot.

named veins

(1) main deep veins of the body

JUGULAR VEINS accompanying the main carotid arteries.

SUBCLAVIAN VEINS from the arms.

With few exceptions the other deep veins lie alongside the arteries already mentioned and have similar names.

UPPER VENA CAVA

PULMONARY VEINS from the lungs.

LOWER VENA CAVA

Blood from the liver passes into large veins that join the LOWER VENA CAVA just before it pierces the diaphragm.

THE LIVER. Here the blood again traverses a rich system of capillaries closely applied to the liver cells. Food products can be removed from the blood and be modified or stored by the liver cells.

VEINS FROM THE ABDOMINAL ORGANS

PORTAL VEIN. The capillaries of the alimentary tract join to form small veins that eventually lead into one large PORTAL VEIN, which enters the liver.

ALIMENTARY SYSTEM

THE MAIN *ILIAC VEINS*, CARRYING BLOOD FROM THE PELVIS AND LOWER LIMBS.

(2) surface veins

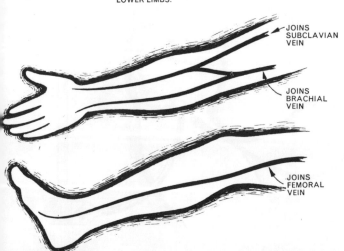

JOINS SUBCLAVIAN VEIN

JOINS BRACHIAL VEIN

Especially in the limbs, there are many veins just beneath the skin. As they approach the heart they dive deeply in to join the main deep vein of the region.

JOINS FEMORAL VEIN

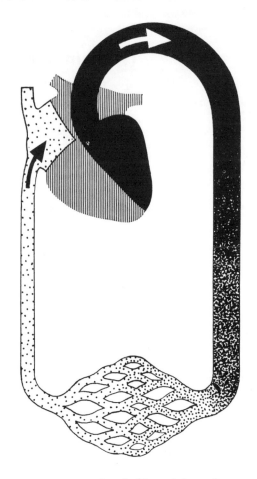

blood pressure

The heart and blood vessels form a closed system with elastic walls. With each beat the heart pumps blood into the pulmonary and systemic circulations (pages 64 and 68). The blood in the arteries is therefore always under pressure but constantly moving onwards. The distribution of blood in the body depends on the degree of contraction of the walls of the small muscular arteries which act like taps (page 66).

measurement of the blood pressure

The pressure of the blood in a main artery of a limb can be measured by applying a hollow, inflatable rubber cuff. The pressure of air which must be pumped into the cuff in order to check the flow of blood through the artery is equal to the blood pressure. The moment when the blood starts to flow again after complete compression of the artery can be detected by listening to the artery just below the cuff.

150

100

50

0 mm Hg

control
of heart and
circulation

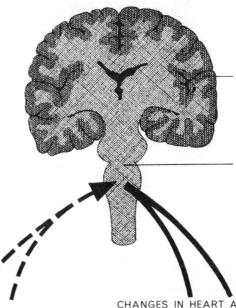

CEREBRUM
note the masses
of neurones
forming the
surface (grey)
matter and the
fluid filled
ventricles

BRAIN STEM

The rate and force of the
heart beat and the opening
and closing of the small
arteries are governed by a
control centre in the brain
stem (page 48).

NERVOUS AND CHEMICAL SIGNALS

CHANGES IN HEART AND ARTERIES
BY OTHER NERVOUS SIGNALS

These mechanisms
control the rate of
circulation of the
blood and its
distribution in relation
to bodily needs.

Resting. Slow pulse –
minimal blood
pressure – small
heart output.

Active. Fast pulse –
higher blood
pressure – large
heart output – most
of the blood now
diverted to the
active muscles.

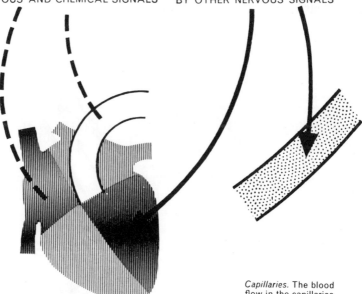

Capillaries. The blood
flow in the capillaries
depends upon the
state of the
small arterial "taps"
that supply them, but
the capillaries are
also widened by the
action of carbon
dioxide and other
waste products of
metabolism upon
their walls.

[75]

blood formation and destruction

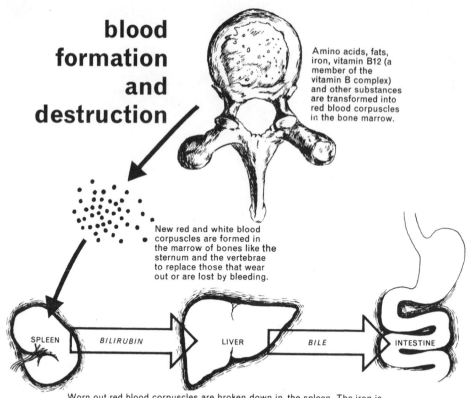

Amino acids, fats, iron, vitamin B12 (a member of the vitamin B complex) and other substances are transformed into red blood corpuscles in the bone marrow.

New red and white blood corpuscles are formed in the marrow of bones like the sternum and the vertebrae to replace those that wear out or are lost by bleeding.

| SPLEEN | *BILIRUBIN* | LIVER | *BILE* | INTESTINE |

Worn out red blood corpuscles are broken down in the spleen. The iron is split from the haemoglobin and stored in the liver while the residue – *bilirubin* – is *excreted* by the liver through the bile duct into the intestine. Bilirubin gives the characteristic colour to the faeces.

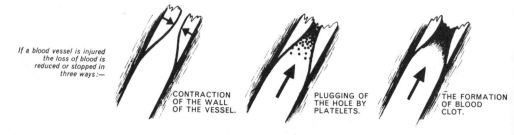

If a blood vessel is injured the loss of blood is reduced or stopped in three ways:—

CONTRACTION OF THE WALL OF THE VESSEL.

PLUGGING OF THE HOLE BY PLATELETS.

THE FORMATION OF BLOOD CLOT.

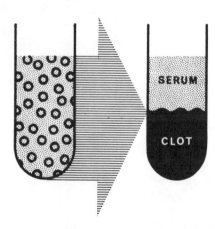

Blood clots after it has been shed because of a complex series of enzyme reactions which changes the *fibrinogen* – a protein dissolved in the blood plasma – into solid *fibrin*. In time the blood clot contracts and yellow *serum* – blood plasma less fibrinogen – is squeezed out.

SERUM

CLOT

blood transfusion

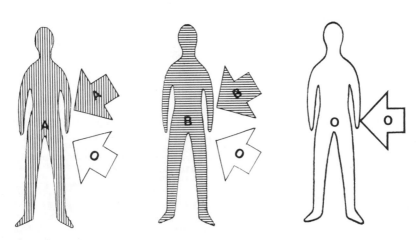

Ill effects or even death may result if blood from one
individual is injected into the circulation
of another. This happens because the defence
mechanisms of the receiver clump the donated red
blood corpuscles together into solid masses which
cause damage by blocking the blood vessels.
To avoid this a special test of the defence
mechanisms – *blood grouping* – is performed.
There are four common blood groups – A, B, AB
and O – and everyone belongs to one of these
groups. Usually an individual can always safely
accept blood from another person having the
same blood group as himself. In practice, blood
transfusion is usually safe in the following
situations.

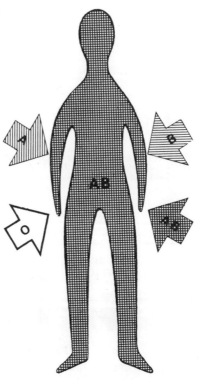

*Another blood group was first discovered in
experiments with Rhesus monkeys. It is also
found in 85% of white people who are then
called Rhesus positive ; the other 15% are Rhesus
negative. The importance of this is that a Rhesus
negative person may be injured by the
transfusion of Rhesus positive blood. A Rhesus
negative woman married to a Rhesus positive
man may conceive a Rhesus positive baby
which can be damaged by a similar type
of reaction.*

*People of the AB blood group, though rare, have
the advantage that they can receive blood from
most other members of the community.*

lymphatic system

The lymphatic system is the drainage system for the tissue spaces, removing excess fluids and particles. Without lymphatics the tissue spaces would slowly become choked with tiny particles of various kinds of material such as free proteins, fat globules, pigment, granules, bacteria and fragments of dead cells. This debris would soon interfere with the normal movement of fluid to and from the blood vessels. Lymphatic vessels in the wall of the small intestine have an additional function; they are important for the absorption and transport of the products of fat digestion from the intestine to the blood stream.

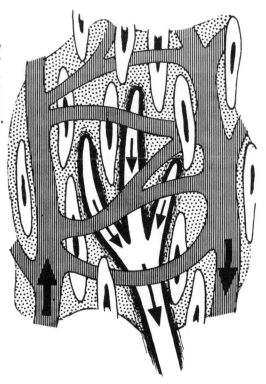

tissue fluid (lymph)

Tissue fluid is formed and reabsorbed automatically in the correct amount by the interplay of several forces. The force exerted by the molecules dissolved in blood and fluid is *osmotic pressure* (page 17).

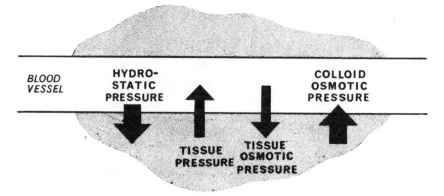

BLOOD VESSEL HYDRO-STATIC PRESSURE COLLOID OSMOTIC PRESSURE TISSUE PRESSURE TISSUE OSMOTIC PRESSURE

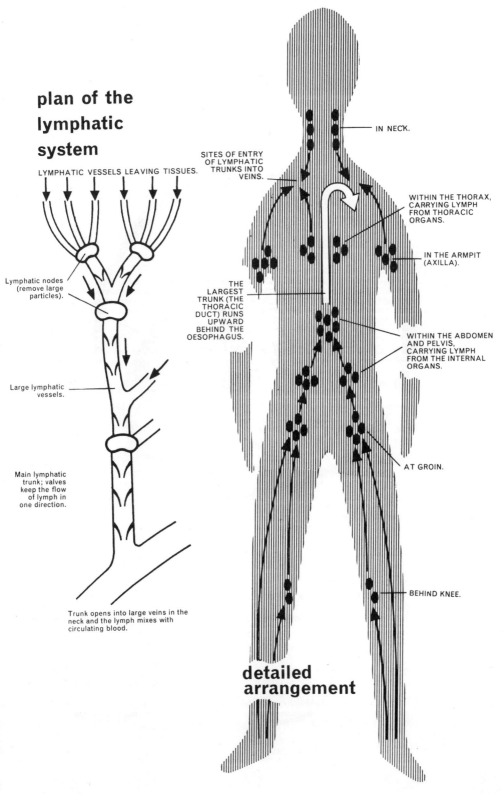

plan of the lymphatic system

LYMPHATIC VESSELS LEAVING TISSUES.

Lymphatic nodes (remove large particles).

Large lymphatic vessels.

Main lymphatic trunk; valves keep the flow of lymph in one direction.

Trunk opens into large veins in the neck and the lymph mixes with circulating blood.

SITES OF ENTRY OF LYMPHATIC TRUNKS INTO VEINS.

IN NECK.

WITHIN THE THORAX, CARRYING LYMPH FROM THORACIC ORGANS.

IN THE ARMPIT (AXILLA).

THE LARGEST TRUNK (THE THORACIC DUCT) RUNS UPWARD BEHIND THE OESOPHAGUS.

WITHIN THE ABDOMEN AND PELVIS, CARRYING LYMPH FROM THE INTERNAL ORGANS.

AT GROIN.

BEHIND KNEE.

detailed arrangement

*The structure and functions of lymphatic nodes are described on page 81.

(1) the skin

The skin – *a waterproof, flexible covering for the whole body.*

VIEW UNDER THE MICROSCOPE

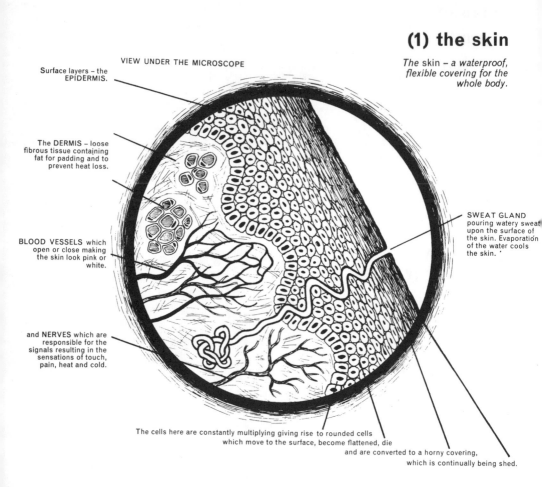

Surface layers – the EPIDERMIS.

The DERMIS – loose fibrous tissue containing fat for padding and to prevent heat loss.

BLOOD VESSELS which open or close making the skin look pink or white.

and NERVES which are responsible for the signals resulting in the sensations of touch, pain, heat and cold.

SWEAT GLAND pouring watery sweat upon the surface of the skin. Evaporation of the water cools the skin. '

The cells here are constantly multiplying giving rise to rounded cells which move to the surface, become flattened, die and are converted to a horny covering, which is continually being shed.

there are certain differences in particular regions

for example :—

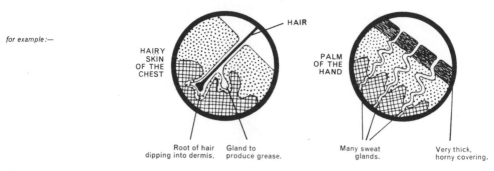

HAIR

HAIRY SKIN OF THE CHEST

PALM OF THE HAND

Root of hair dipping into dermis.

Gland to produce grease.

Many sweat glands.

Very thick, horny covering.

(2) the filtering mechanism

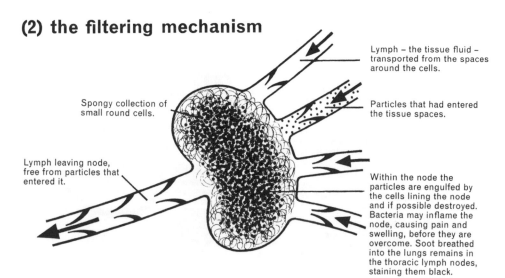

Lymph – the tissue fluid – transported from the spaces around the cells.

Spongy collection of small round cells.

Particles that had entered the tissue spaces.

Lymph leaving node, free from particles that entered it.

Within the node the particles are engulfed by the cells lining the node and if possible destroyed. Bacteria may inflame the node, causing pain and swelling, before they are overcome. Soot breathed into the lungs remains in the thoracic lymph nodes, staining them black.

The LYMPHATIC NODES (or GLANDS) are important filters of the tissue fluid should any particles (especially bacteria) enter through a crack in the skin.

(3) antibody production

The lymphatic nodes and certain organs of similar structure also manufacture chemicals that help the body to withstand a second "invasion" by particular kinds of bacteria. These organs include the tonsils (page 60) the THYMUS lying behind the sternum and the SPLEEN.

In addition the spleen assists the liver in producing bile pigment from aged red blood corpuscles. It sends the pigment to the liver in the portal vein, for *excretion* along the bile duct into the intestine (page 76).

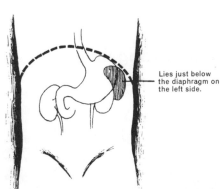

Lies just below the diaphragm on the left side.

(4) engulfing by white blood cells

Most white blood cells are able to engulf particles, notably bacteria. Collections of such cells constitute *pus*.

principles

The waste products from the cells pass into the circulating blood. The carbon dioxide is given off within the lungs (page 55). The other substances pass in the blood through the kidneys where they are removed from the blood and discharged from the body excreted in the urine.

RENAL ARTERY

RENAL VEIN

ideal arrangement

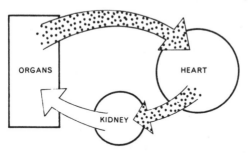

ORGANS

HEART

KIDNEY

Ideally all the blood leaving the heart should pass through the kidneys before reaching the other organs.

actual arrangement

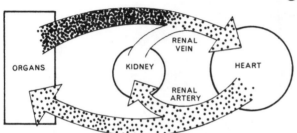

ORGANS

KIDNEY

RENAL VEIN

RENAL ARTERY

HEART

The actual arrangement does not allow complete removal of waste products from the blood reaching the organs, but the amounts normally circulating are too small to do harm even to the sensitive cells of the nervous system.

details

A kidney is made up of many units, the *kidney tubules,* each bearing a rounded expansion that acts as a sieve. The expanded portion forms a partial covering for a twisted mass of capillaries and is known as Bowman's capsule. Blood circulates through the kidney at the rate of 2 pints per minute in vessels that pass into close association with the tubules after leaving Bowman's capsule.

Blood enters the kidney at high pressure through the renal artery.

CAPILLARIES

BOWMAN'S CAPSULE

} Both lined by flattened,

permeable cells.

Process of filtering all small molecules from the blood.

Water and substance made of *small* molecules exude in the tubule.

} Water, glucose. sodium chloride and other salts. Waste products.

Highly concentrated blood remaining in the capillary blood vessels.

Process of reabsorbing into the blood all substances valuable to the body.

Water, glucose, Most salts.

} Pass *back* into the blood from the tubule.

Fluid in the tubule now contains mainly waste products (especially *urea* and *uric acid*) dissolved in water. This is URINE.

Blood restored to its original dilution, but without waste products, returns from the kidneys in the *renal vein*.

Concentrated *urine* leaves the kidney.

discharge of urine

The kidney tubules are coiled and twisted together. Each discharges its share of urine into the funnel-shaped top of the *ureter*.

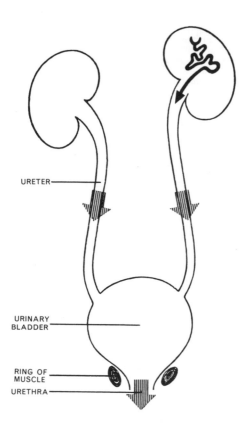

URETER—

URINARY
BLADDER—

RING OF
MUSCLE—
URETHRA—

The urine collects in the muscular — walled *urinary bladder* which empties at intervals through the outlet tube, the *urethra*. When the bladder is full, signals pass down the nerves to the bladder making its walls contract and the ring of muscles around the urethra relax. Urination is an automatic process in the young child but in later life it comes under the control of the will.

In the *male*, the urethra passes through a large gland, the *prostate*, before running inside the *penis*.

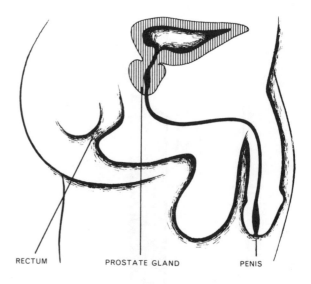

RECTUM   PROSTATE GLAND   PENIS

regulation of body fluids

In addition to removing waste products from the blood, the kidney helps to regulate the volume, acidity and composition of the blood and therefore of the tissue fluids. The kidney tubules are able to respond to chemicals, acting as "messengers", that reach them in the blood coming from the *pituitary* and *adrenal* glands (page 86).

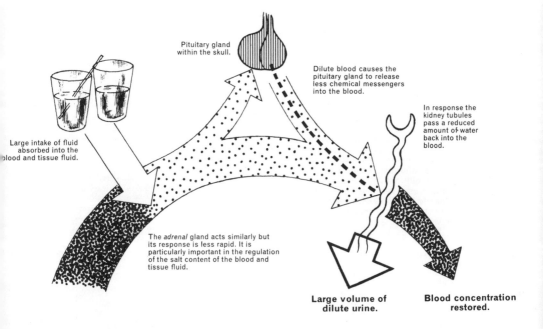

Pituitary gland within the skull.

Dilute blood causes the pituitary gland to release less chemical messengers into the blood.

In response the kidney tubules pass a reduced amount of water back into the blood.

Large intake of fluid absorbed into the blood and tissue fluid.

The *adrenal* gland acts similarly but its response is less rapid. It is particularly important in the regulation of the salt content of the blood and tissue fluid.

Large volume of dilute urine.

Blood concentration restored.

differs in the two sexes

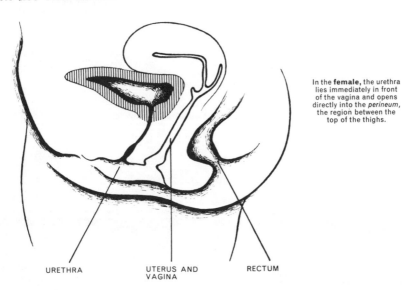

In the **female,** the urethra lies immediately in front of the vagina and opens directly into the *perineum*, the region between the top of the thighs.

URETHRA   UTERUS AND VAGINA   RECTUM

endocrine system

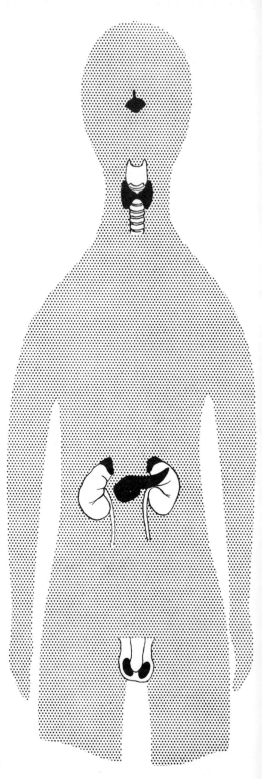

Many bodily activities are controlled or influenced by chemical messengers carried in the blood stream. These messengers – *hormones* – are made by special organs called *endocrine glands*. The alternative name *ductless glands* is often used because the hormones pass directly into the blood instead of running in ducts. Some of these glands especially the *pituitary* and *adrenal* produce numerous hormones with very complex activities. Others are relatively simple – like the *thyroid* – but their hormones may still profoundly influence every cell in the body. The endocrine glands and their hormones are responsible for much of the smooth running of the body and co-operation between the various systems. The processes and systems affected include metabolism, circulation, heat production, growth, response to infection or other stress, maintenance of the correct levels and amounts of fluid, salts, sugar and proteins. Disease or removal of the endocrine glands causes severe disturbances of bodily functions.

pituitary gland

FRONT PART OF GLAND (ANTERIOR LOBE)

Influences growth of all cells
,,   adrenal gland
,,   thyroid gland
,,   reproductive glands

BACK PART OF GLAND (POSTERIOR LOBE)

Influences blood vessels
,,   kidney (page 85)

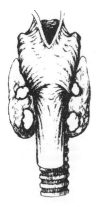

thyroid gland

Produces thyroxine which controls the rate of metabolic (chemical) activity in all the cells of the body. Thyroxine is essential for normal physical and mental development in the child.

parathyroid gland

Produces *parathormone* which controls the calcium and phosphorus metabolism, and therefore the state of the bones, in the body.

pancreas

Special islands of cells (Islands of Langerhans) produce *insulin* which controls the utilisation of sugar by the body (page 88).

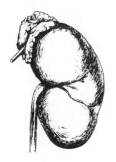

adrenal gland

Cortex produces several hormones which control the metabolism of sodium, chlorine, protein and, partly, carbohydrate in the body. *Medulla* produces *adrenaline* which augments the activity of the sympathetic nervous system upon the heart, circulation and carbohydrate metabolism.

sex gland

The testis and ovary secrete hormones which are essential for normal sexual development and reproduction.

blood sugar

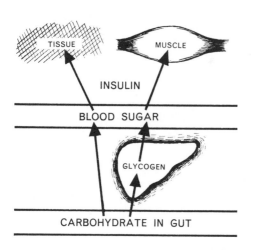

The level of glucose in the blood depends upon the amount absorbed from the intestine and the amount delivered to the tissues. The tissues use glucose for energy and any surplus is either stored in the muscles and liver as glycogen or is converted to fat. Insulin, from the pancreas, controls the entry of glucose into the cells. A rise in blood sugar evokes a secretion of insulin which reduces the level. A fall in blood sugar stops insulin secretion and mobilises glucose from the glycogen stores. Fat is stored beneath the skin and around or between the organs.

temperature

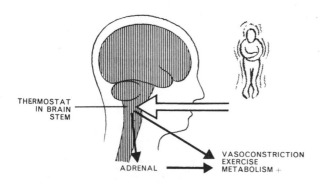

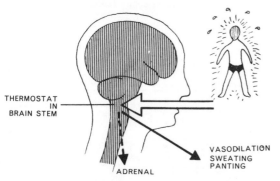

Complex reactions keep the body temperature steady between 36 and 37 C. A nerve centre in the brain stem responds like a thermostat to changes in the temperature of the blood reaching it.

Cooling evokes nerve signals which shut off the blood supply to the skin and this reduces the heat dissipated from its surface. They also increase the rate of metabolism of the body and cause shivering - rapid muscular contractions producing heat. The signals act both directly and by stimulating the adrenal glands.

Heating the body cuts off the secretion of adrenaline, opens up the skin circulation and causes sweating so that the body is cooled by radiation and evaporation.

regulation

acid-base balance
acidaemia

All the chemical processes in the body cause the continual pouring out of acid waste products and carbon dioxide into the tissue fluid (page 11). This tends to produce *acidaemia* which could soon poison the cells of the body. The blood and tissue fluids neutralise and absorb these poisons by means of chemicals which are said to act as *buffers* – bicarbonate, phosphate and protein. The poisons are eliminated by the lungs; liver and kidneys.

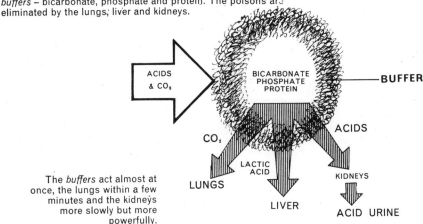

The *buffers* act almost at once, the lungs within a few minutes and the kidneys more slowly but more powerfully.

alkalaemia

Occasionally, because of vomiting, illness or the use of drugs the body may be short of acid giving a tendency to *alkalaemia*. The same buffer mechanisms deal with this. Breathing becomes shallow to conserve carbon dioxide and the kidneys produce an alkaline* urine.
Alkalies (bases) are neutralisers of acids; they turn red litmus paper blue.

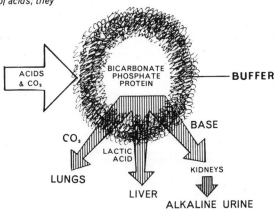

section three **the product of the human body**

The products of most factories emerge complete and ready for use. The only object that human bodies produce - a newborn baby - is small and unable to exist alone; it must rely on others to provide food, clothing, protection and guidance for many years. During childhood the body grows by the multiplication rather than by the enlargement of its cells. Growth is complete by 25 years but the various organs and systems develop at different rates, so that a person can become a parent (achieve sexual maturity) long before the skeleton has stopped growing. The products of a factory are standardised and identical. Except for identical twins, all babies differ from each other, inheriting their appearance and other attributes, including racial characteristics, from their parents. Subsequently, their development and behaviour can be modified by the circumstances around them. The interaction of the two forces of heredity and environment produces the vast diversity of the human population of the world.

The father and mother participate in the production of a new human being

reproduction

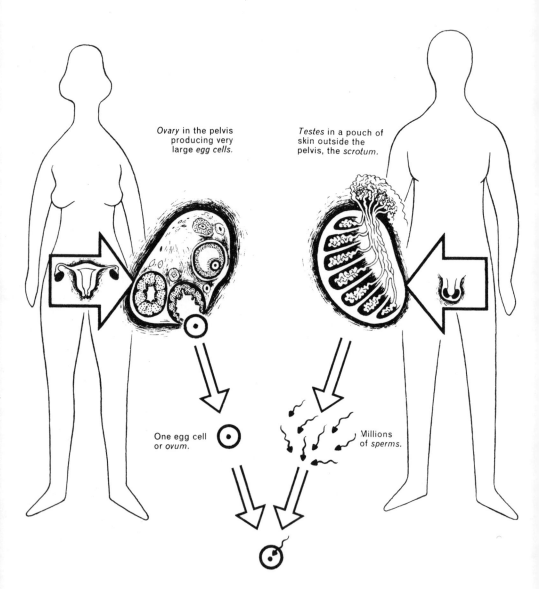

Ovary in the pelvis producing very large *egg cells*.

Testes in a pouch of skin outside the pelvis, the *scrotum*.

One egg cell or *ovum*.

Millions of *sperms*.

Fertilization of ovum by a single sperm.

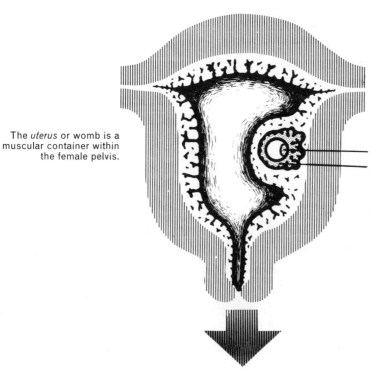

The *uterus* or womb is a muscular container within the female pelvis.

Divides into millions of cells to form:—

An *embryo* and

membranes around the embryo.

They grow and are nourished within the uterus.

After three months the embryo begins to resemble a human being and is called a foetus.

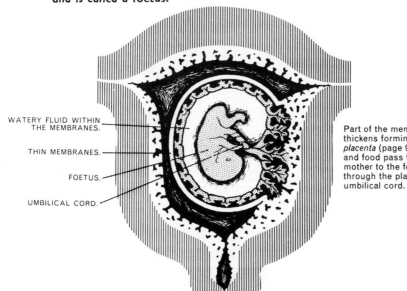

WATERY FLUID WITHIN THE MEMBRANES.

THIN MEMBRANES.

FOETUS.

UMBILICAL CORD.

Part of the membranes thickens forming the *placenta* (page 97). Oxygen and food pass from the mother to the foetus through the placenta and umbilical cord.

After nine calendar months the foetus is expelled as a baby.

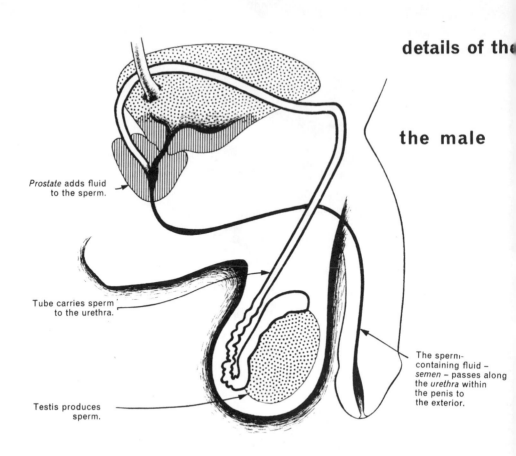

Prostate adds fluid to the sperm.

Tube carries sperm to the urethra.

Testis produces sperm.

The sperm-containing fluid – *semen* – passes along the *urethra* within the penis to the exterior.

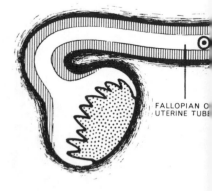

FALLOPIAN O
UTERINE TUBE

passage for the sperm

Production of ova. Every 28 days one ovum bursts out of the ovary and passes along the uterine tube.

reproduction (cont.)

reproductive system

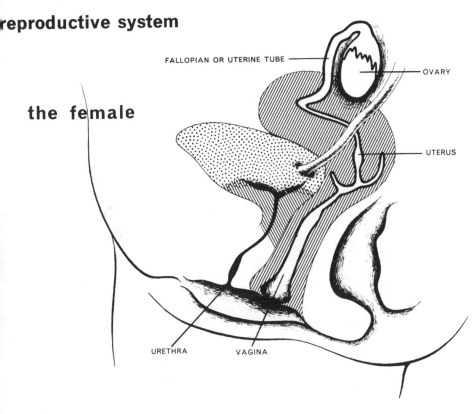

the female

FALLOPIAN OR UTERINE TUBE

OVARY

UTERUS

URETHRA   VAGINA

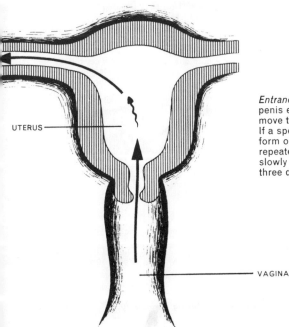

UTERUS

VAGINA

Entrance of the sperm. In sexual intercourse the penis expels semen into the *vagina.* The sperms move through the uterus into the uterine tubes. If a sperm meets an ovum the two combine to form one cell – the *fertilized ovum.* This divides repeatedly forming a growing mass of cells. This slowly moves into the uterus during the next three days and becomes attached to its wall.

the muscular wall of
the uterus has
a cellular lining
which continually changes
in thickness, partly
in response to hormones
produced by the ovary.

hormones and the reproductive system

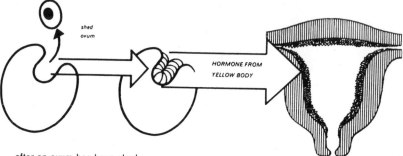

after an ovum has been shed . . .

the "shell" produces new cells and forms
the *yellow body* a temporary endocrine
gland that acts upon the uterus.

lining of
the uterus is
made to thicken.

subsequent changes depend on whether the shed ovum was *fertilized*

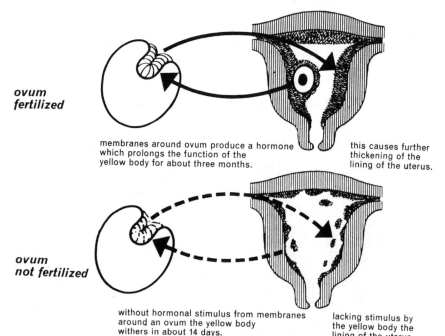

*ovum
fertilized*

membranes around ovum produce a hormone
which prolongs the function of the
yellow body for about three months.

this causes further
thickening of the
lining of the uterus.

*ovum
not fertilized*

without hormonal stimulus from membranes
around an ovum the yellow body
withers in about 14 days.

lacking stimulus by
the yellow body the
lining of the uterus
breaks down.

*The fragmented uterine lining is shed every month as the
"menstrual flow". These "periods" of tissue loss stop during pregnancy.*

nourishment of the young

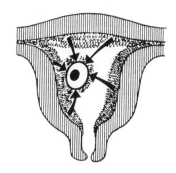

the embryo and foetus

For the first few days, the lining
of the uterus supplies essential
food material which is absorbed
through the thin membranes
covering the embryo.

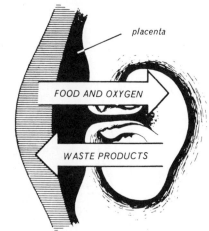

placenta

FOOD AND OXYGEN

WASTE PRODUCTS

Later, one part of the membranes
becomes greatly thickened and
develops thin walled blood vessels.
These lie close to the mother's
blood vessels in the wall of the
uterus, allowing free interchange
of food, gases and waste products
between the two circulations.
This thickened region of contact
is called the *placenta*.

after birth

Shortly after the birth the
placenta is itself expelled from
the uterus as the "after birth".
The newborn infant is suckled for
some months at the breast which
has enlarged during pregnancy and
now begins to secrete milk.

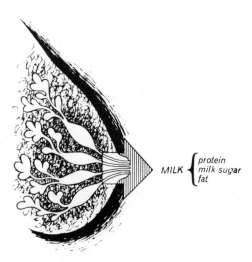

MILK { protein
milk sugar
fat

An 8 lb. baby requires a pint of
breast milk per day.

If cow's milk has to be given instead,
water and sugar must be added to
bring its composition near to
that of breast milk.

boy or girl

although all sperms look alike there are two
functional types. One—which can be called
type X—causes the fertilised ovum to grow
into a girl; the other—type Y—causes it to
become a boy. All ova are identical—type X.
Thus all women are made up of cells that result
from the union of an X sperm and the
X ovum. All men are made up of cells resulting
from the union of a Y sperm with the X ovum.

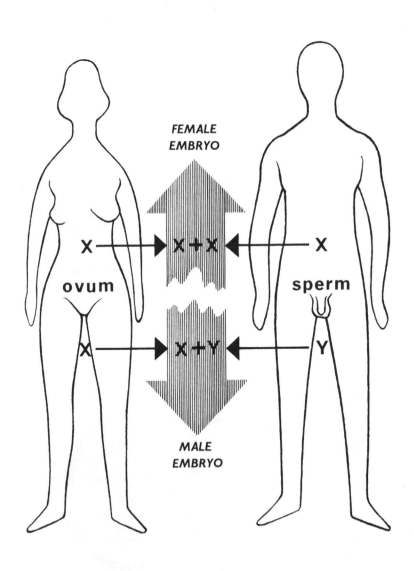

FEMALE
EMBRYO

X → X+X ← X

ovum   sperm

X → X+Y ← Y

MALE
EMBRYO

twins

**there are
two types.**

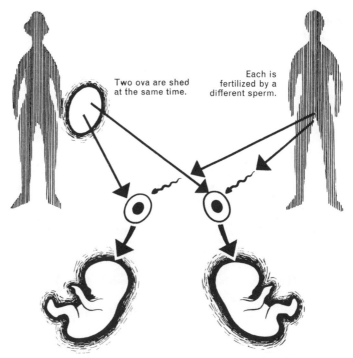

Two ova are shed
at the same time.

Each is
fertilized by a
different sperm.

non identical   *two different embryos*

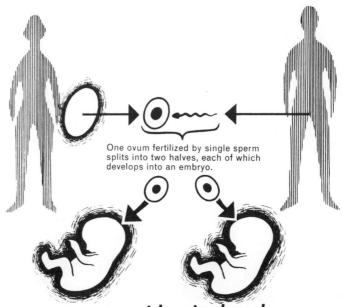

One ovum fertilized by single sperm
splits into two halves, each of which
develops into an embryo.

identical   *two identical embryos*

A newborn infant, weighing 7-8 lbs., is not just a scaled down version of an adult. The differences in proportion are shown below.

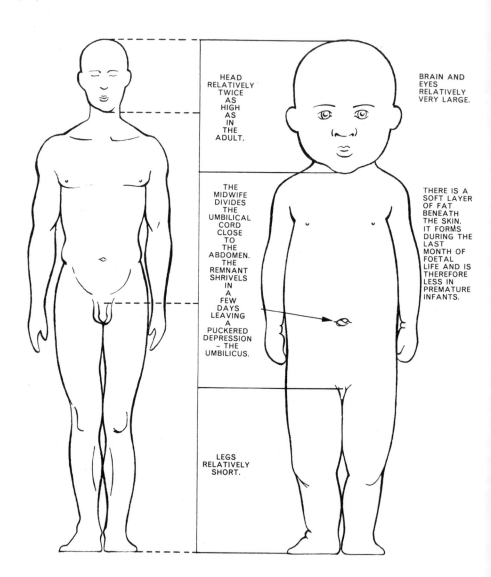

HEAD RELATIVELY TWICE AS HIGH AS IN THE ADULT.

BRAIN AND EYES RELATIVELY VERY LARGE.

THE MIDWIFE DIVIDES THE UMBILICAL CORD CLOSE TO THE ABDOMEN. THE REMNANT SHRIVELS IN A FEW DAYS LEAVING A PUCKERED DEPRESSION – THE UMBILICUS.

THERE IS A SOFT LAYER OF FAT BENEATH THE SKIN. IT FORMS DURING THE LAST MONTH OF FOETAL LIFE AND IS THEREFORE LESS IN PREMATURE INFANTS.

LEGS RELATIVELY SHORT.

other characteristic features are :—

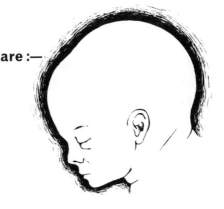

the skeleton

Some actual *compression* of the skull can occur because the bones are separated by gaps filled in by membranes. The large gap on top of the head remains open for more than a year.

The head is moulded into this form by pressure within the mother's vagina during birth. It regains its proper shape in a few hours.

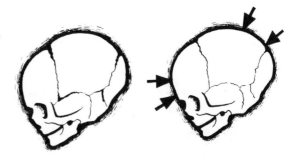

the spine

The spine is curved and the limbs at rest are bent up. The soles of the feet face toward each other.

other organs

The stomach is small and only able to digest milk. The infant may look rather yellow for a few days because the liver cannot at first dispose of bile pigments fast enough. The heart beats very rapidly – about 120 per minute before birth falling to about 100 per minute in the next week or two.
Many of the nerve tracts in the brain and spinal cord are imperfectly formed. The newborn infant sleeps for most of the 24 hours.

growth

Most tissues, for example cartilage, can grow by division of the cells and the production of new matrix between them.

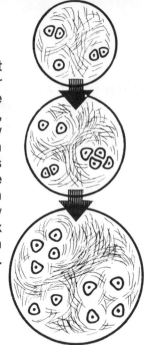

Bones and teeth are rigid so that the contained cells are not able to spread apart.

growth of bones

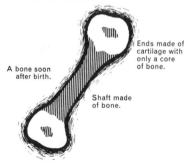

A bone soon after birth.

Ends made of cartilage with only a core of bone.

Shaft made of bone.

By the early twenties, the growth of the cartilage has finished and all the masses of bone join together.

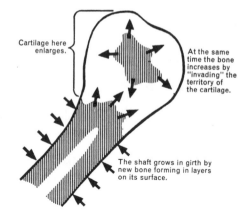

Cartilage here enlarges.

At the same time the bone increases by "invading" the territory of the cartilage.

The shaft grows in girth by new bone forming in layers on its surface.

development of teeth

Between 6 months and two years the milk teeth come through the gums. This is the "teething period"

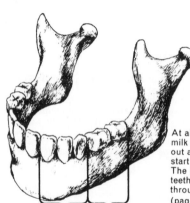

At about 6 years the milk teeth begin to fall out and the adult teeth start to come through. The last, the wisdom teeth, are usually through by 17 years. (page 29).

total 4 × (3 biting + 2 grinding) = 20 milk teeth

landmarks in childhood

*There is much varia-
bility. These graphs
refer to an average
child.*

landmarks
during
infancy

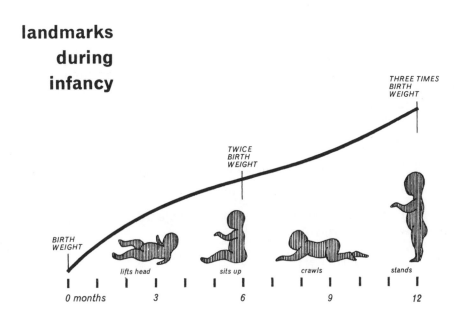

THREE TIMES
BIRTH
WEIGHT

TWICE
BIRTH
WEIGHT

BIRTH
WEIGHT

| lifts head | sits up | crawls | stands |

0 months 3 6 9 12

landmarks
in childhood
and adolescence

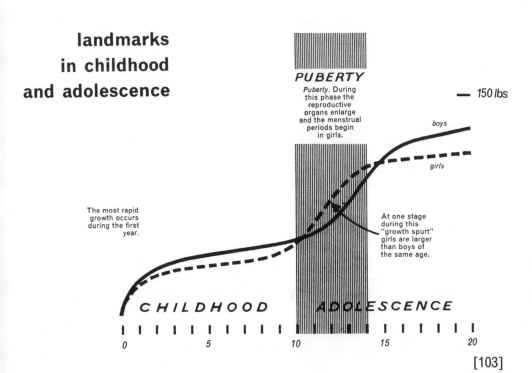

PUBERTY

Puberty. During
this phase the
reproductive
organs enlarge
and the menstrual
periods begin
in girls.

— 150 lbs

boys

girls

The most rapid
growth occurs
during the first
year.

At one stage
during this
"growth spurt"
girls are larger
than boys of
the same age.

CHILDHOOD　　*ADOLESCENCE*

0　　　5　　　10　　　15　　　20

ageing

AGEING Characteristic changes occur in the ageing human body. Some—for example, the skin and arteries—can be attributed partly to the loss of elasticity. Others—as in the joints—result from wear and tear and still others may be due to failure of certain ductless glands to produce adequate hormones. As the body fails, the lessening of mental and physical activity lead to further deterioration. Common changes are:—

Hair loses colour and is often lost.

Powers of learning and concentration reduced.

Hearing and other senses often deteriorate.

Lens of eye cannot focus on near objects.

Skin sags and wrinkles form.

Teeth lost.

Rib cartilages lose elasticity.

The intervertebral discs degenerate.

The bones become brittle.

Joint surfaces become rough and irregular.

Digestion is often impaired.

The arteries become more rigid.

Reproductive powers diminish. In women the discharge of ova stops entirely at menopause.

In men the prostate enlarges and may obstruct the urethra.

death

In a young person the maintenance systems (page 26) are more than adequate to keep all the cells healthy. For example, one kidney or one lung can be removed without seriously impairing the excretory or the respiratory systems respectively.

In the aged, one or more of these systems becomes inefficient. The circulatory system (page 64) is a key one; if it fails, the cells of the body are imperfectly nourished and cannot rid themselves of their waste products. If the flow of blood through the coronary arteries or the arteries to the brain ceases, even temporarily, death may ensue—a "heart attack" or a "stroke". Some cells can survive for hours even if their supply of blood is cut off, but the brain cells die if deprived of blood for more than a few minutes. Once the circulation has ceased permanently, the accumulation of waste products within all the cells leads to their death. The tissues are soon invaded by bacteria and other small animals and eventually only the non-living matter of the bone matrix is left.

the
arrangement
of the
organs

The main organs of the body have now been described as components of individual systems. Students desiring to extend their knowledge will wish to know how the organs fit together within the thorax and abdomen.

There are so many organs that they cannot all be represented on one picture and the reader must therefore cut out some of the following figures if he wishes to understand fully the internal arrangement of the body.

Begin by studying the diagram of the heart on the opposite page and confirm that it accurately shows the circulation through the right and left sides of the heart. After removing the page along the dotted line, cut out this diagram and also the lower figure; then gum or paste them accurately back to back. Fold the model as shown in the small pictures to produce a correctly shaped heart.

reproduced fror
Medical and Biological Illustratio
by permission of the edito

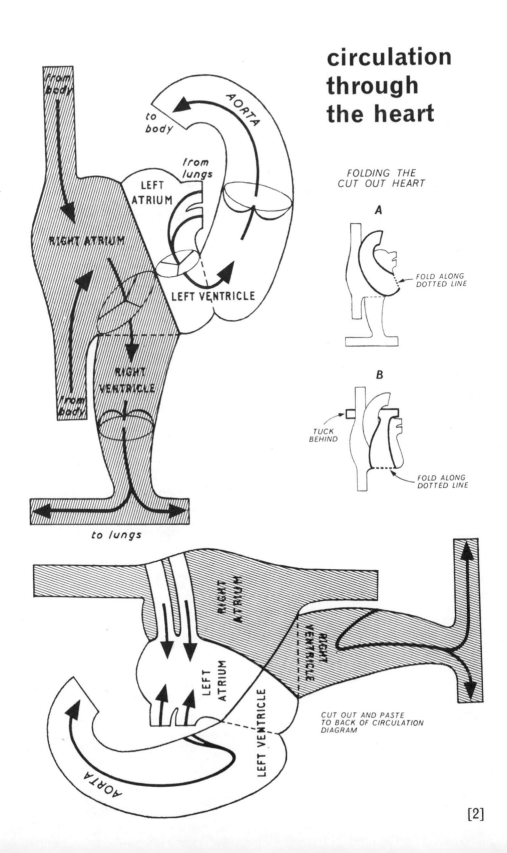

circulation through the heart

FOLDING THE
CUT OUT HEART

A

FOLD ALONG
DOTTED LINE

B

TUCK
BEHIND

FOLD ALONG
DOTTED LINE

from body

AORTA

to body

from lungs

LEFT ATRIUM

RIGHT ATRIUM

LEFT VENTRICLE

from body

RIGHT VENTRICLE

to lungs

RIGHT ATRIUM

RIGHT VENTRICLE

LEFT ATRIUM

LEFT VENTRICLE

AORTA

CUT OUT AND PASTE
TO BACK OF CIRCULATION
DIAGRAM

the arrangement of the organs (cont.)

On the opposite page is represented the interior of the chest after the heart (and its covering bag, the pericardium) has been removed. By superimposing the model heart upon this figure one can restore the complete layout of the thoracic organs and understand what is in contact with the back and sides of the heart. Its front is covered by the front part of the chest wall.

the thorax

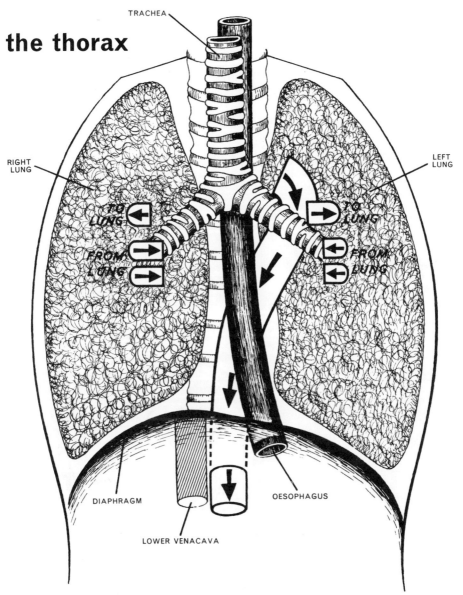

TRACHEA

RIGHT LUNG

LEFT LUNG

TO LUNG

TO LUNG

FROM LUNG

FROM LUNG

DIAPHRAGM

LOWER VENACAVA

OESOPHAGUS

note: the bottom of this picture corresponds to the top of that on page 8.

the abdomen

All the abdominal organs are supplied with blood by branches of the aorta, which runs vertically down in front of the bodies of the vertebrae. Certain organs are loosely fixed to the back wall of the abdomen. Others lie further forward and are freely movable. Their mobility is limited only by the arteries tethering them to the aorta.

The walls of the abdomen, including its domed roof, the diaphragm, are lined by a thin membrane called the *peritoneum*. This passes across the front of the *fixed* organs and their arteries. It clothes both sides of the arteries running to the *mobile* organs and then surrounds the organs themselves. The double layer of peritoneum enclosing blood vessels to an organ is called a *mesentery*.

These relationships can best be understood by studying a cross-section of the abdomen.

BACK

FIXED ORGAN

AORTA

MESENTERY

MOBILE ORGAN

ABDOMINAL WALL

FRONT

The pictures on the next two right hand pages show the organs that have mesenteries and the fixed organs respectively. The rectangles on page 6 should be cut out to show the way the main organs are grouped within the abdomen.

the abdominal organs that are movable

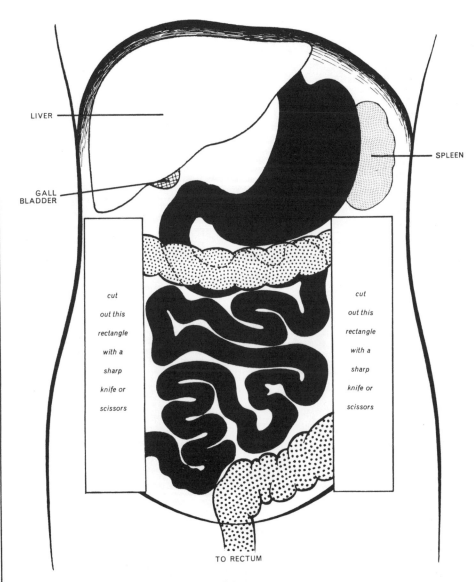

LIVER

SPLEEN

GALL BLADDER

cut out this rectangle with a sharp knife or scissors

cut out this rectangle with a sharp knife or scissors

TO RECTUM

cut along this line

The oesophagus, stomach and small intestine are shown in black. The large intestine is shown stippled.

stick this edge to the top of page opposite

do not apply any paste or gum below the dotted line

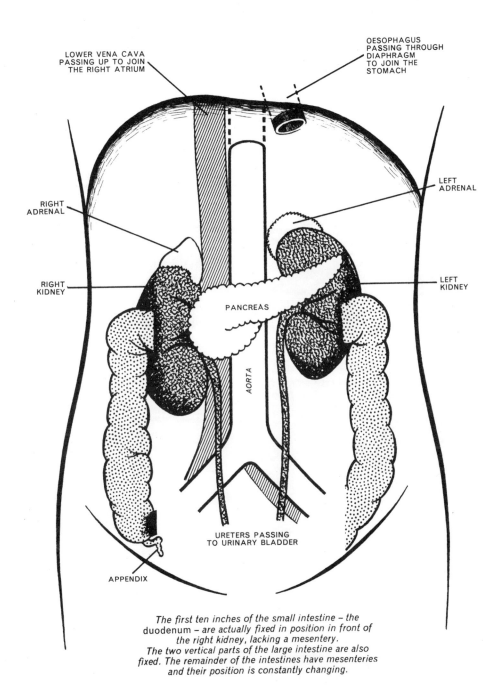

LOWER VENA CAVA
PASSING UP TO JOIN
THE RIGHT ATRIUM

OESOPHAGUS
PASSING THROUGH
DIAPHRAGM
TO JOIN THE
STOMACH

RIGHT
ADRENAL

LEFT
ADRENAL

RIGHT
KIDNEY

LEFT
KIDNEY

PANCREAS

AORTA

URETERS PASSING
TO URINARY BLADDER

APPENDIX

*The first ten inches of the small intestine – the
duodenum – are actually fixed in position in front of
the right kidney, lacking a mesentery.
The two vertical parts of the large intestine are also
fixed. The remainder of the intestines have mesenteries
and their position is constantly changing.*

[8]

index